sunday ink

WORKS BY THE UPTOWN WRITERS

Carol Bolt

Pamela Hobart Carter

Geri Gale

Sandra E. Jones

Susan Knox

Stacy Lawson

Arleen Williams

Janet Yoder

Sunday Ink
Works by the Uptown Writers

By Carol Bolt, Pamela Hobart Carter, Geri Gale, Sandra E. Jones,
Susan Knox, Stacy Lawson, Arleen Williams, and Janet Yoder

"The Disorder" originally appeared in *Bayou Magazine,* Issue 43, 2004,
and *StringTown Magazine*, Issue 7, 2004.

Edited by Waverly Fitzgerald.
Proofreading by Geri Gale.
Design by Pamela Farrington.
Cover design by Carol Bolt.
ISBN: 145283542X

Tasseomancy Press, Seattle
The Uptown Writers
2021 First Avenue G-18
Seattle, WA 98121 USA
www.areleenwilliams.com
Email: aw@arleenwilliams.com

Printed on recycled acid-free paper.

dedication

Marie Worley Unkefer (1915–2003)

Winifred R. Shackleford (c. 1916–)

Skagit tribal treasure, Vi Hilbert taqʷšəblu (1918-2008)

Poet, Irene Drennan (1922-2008)

Southport Island sailing teacher, Norma Smith (1927–)

Lois Hirshkowitz (1936–2008)

Patricia Calderon (1960–2002)

Maureen Feeney (1963–1983)

foreword

Pat Takayama and Diana Taylor met to
write at Teahouse Kuan Yin in Seattle's
Wallingford neighborhood on a Sunday
morning in 1991. Pat had studied with
Natalie Goldberg, author of *Writing Down
the Bones*. Both Pat and Diana had studied
with Robert Ray in Seattle who reinforced
those bones. So Pat and Diana launched
a writing group to practice what they had
learned, to practice writing by doing
writing practice.

Natalie Goldberg's rules of writing
practice are:

1) Keep your hand moving.

2) Don't cross out.

*3) Don't worry about spelling, punctuation,
or grammar (or editing).*

4) Lose control.

5) Don't think. Don't get logical.

6) Go for the jugular (where the scary energy is).

Over time new members joined and some
departed. Each Sunday we writers visited
over pots of steaming Assam, Darjeeling,
Oolong, or Sencha. We set the timer and
wrote together, pens scrawling across
pages in a race with time. When the timer
beeped, the pens stopped. Then each in
turn read aloud the words she had just
written. We listened to each other and
to ourselves.

When the teahouse no longer served
our needs, we moved to Uptown Espresso
on Fourth Avenue in Belltown and then to
Uptown Espresso on Westlake, where the
old library tables are large and far enough
apart to give us the feeling we have landed
in our own expansive place. Rich espresso
replaced exotic teas. Still the group remains
a compelling Sunday refuge.

Why do we writers meet?
Why write together?
Why fall silent to listen to each one read?
Why do we continue to do this each
Sunday over the course of years, almost
two decades?

It is the magic of not knowing what we will
write, of surprising ourselves with words—
words on Thelonious Monk, on being in
the world of a Skagit tribal elder, on the
aunt who smokes while wheezily dragging
her oxygen tank behind like a pet dog,
on Irish sisters who follow diverse paths,
on the unhinged door of a newly opened
life, on a hand-sanded dinghy, on revised
fairy tales, on vibrators, on remembrance,
on breast cancer, on affairs, on radiation
exposure at Hanford, on memory and
its loss, secrets, quirks, love, fear, anger,
obsession, and death. The longer we write
together, the deeper the writing, and the
deeper the connections among us.

We have forged a sense of each other's strengths and sensitivities both on and off the page. We are a table of writers committed to pursuing literary arts in an open, safe, and respectful setting.

Each Sunday we meet to write, then soak up each other's words, laughter, tears, and encouragement. We fill notebooks, then more notebooks with energetic efforts, surprising new words, raw material to take to the next level. Welcome to *Sunday Ink: Works by the Uptown Writers*—our book, an outpouring of our writing together.

contents

introduction

We are a city of readers and writers. And many of us Seattleites are "writing-practice writers" who meet at one or another café, who, supplied with the essential espresso, set a kitchen timer and commence to write in a notebook for a half-hour without pause or correction. When the timer goes off, the writers read around the table, read the raw writing without critique or comment, then reset the timer and return to writing. Exercising memory and imagination and the writing hand. Here is a way to access the material one is given to write. A way to get productive and stay that way. A way to write pieces or chapters or scenes. A way to keep writing when time evaporates or when "life" intervenes. In this world of writing practice, the term "writer's block" is not bandied about because quite simply it does not occur. After a session you take your notebook home and you type out what you have written and then you have something to work on, to revise, to compose and recompose.

Sunday Ink gathers works of eight Seattle-based writers who have been writing together in this way for almost two decades. The book is a mosaic of fiction, poetry, memoir, and a play, and it includes both narrative and non-narrative forms. The pieces are short—readable during work breaks or before bed. I found it satisfying to dip into the volume a bit at a time.

Carol Bolt offers two New England marine memoirs, one by way of apology to lobsters restless in the bucket carrying them to their fate as someone's dinner; the other a paean to an antique wooden sailboat that stood as an emblem of childhood happiness.

Pamela Hobart Carter's play *Unhinged* explores the tension between making art and making dinner, a conflict that appears to be unhinging a marriage. The artist/wife removes the door between kitchen and garden and the question is: was this an act of creative liberation or a symptom of becoming unhinged? Or is it her conventional husband who is becoming unhinged?

Geri Gale's poems also engage the realm of personal and creative freedom. The poems carry us quite away from "this make-everything-clear-and-easy era." In "Zero through Nine" history is:

> ... a nightmare I try to wake from
>
> my freedom hinges
>
> upon the last king being strangled
>
> with the entrails of the last priest.

This is a love poem of sorts, in which the lover takes:

> ... all the necessary
>
> (horrible and very lovely) steps
>
> pass white picket fence
>
> pass car-spitting pistons
>
> past girdled grace and windless steadfast.

The person, the finally individuated soul, arrives at her own self:

> for this is my time our time in time
>
> to join my body rune-rime.

Susan Knox and **Arleen Williams** each present parallel, powerful, tender accounts of mothers sinking into dementia. "Years ago," writes Knox, "I used to tease Mom when she was worried about getting Alzheimer's. I told her it wouldn't matter if she got it because she wouldn't know. But she does know. I didn't know that she would know. She knows." Williams takes her mother out for a drive. Her mother tells her she is a good driver. She tells her mother she had good teachers. Her mother asks, "Who?" Williams answers, "You and Dad taught me, remember?" And then reflects, "I realize my mistake before the word is out of my mouth. Like a slap in the face, I used the word *remember*. I tested her memory. She clams up, desperately trying to *remember*. I keep talking, determined to explain away her confusion."

Sandra E. Jones also opens up the worlds that families inhabit. She brings us into vivid contact with a fine-crafted two-seated outhouse that served as library and reading room for a child and her ingenious and kindly grandfather. Memorable characters include the outhouse itself, interior-decorated in blue and hung with a child's framed paintings. In another piece Jones gives us her theatrical Aunt Sue's hilarious rendition of her own death, and later, the wholly unfunny death itself.

In "Putting on the Dog," **Stacy Lawson** weaves the two bright threads of clothes and God, or is it clothes and the divided devotions of those who wear them? Is your T-shirt too tight and according to whom? Have you become tangled in your aging wedding dress on your way to celebrating Purim and your anniversary? Does the Torah, too, need to be stitched, patched, and indeed, dressed? Lawson executes this prismatic and perceptive reflection in the lovely form of the titled theme piece.

Finally we come to **Janet Yoder**'s lyrical, majestic memoir of the Skagit elder Vi Hilbert, a memoir centered on the Healing Heart Symphony commissioned by Hilbert, composed by Bruce Ruddell, and played by the Seattle Symphony Orchestra. Vi Hilbert considered her life work—to preserve the Lushootseed language and the culture of her people—as an assignment from the other side. To further the work she freely gave out assignments to others, assignments that became powerful incentives to continue the work. Janet Yoder's assignment was to help preserve Vi's legacy (in various ways) and this creative nonfiction represents part of this obligation. It is a fitting close to this offering from the Uptown Writers group.

Stories must be told, as Arleen Williams states in her piece on writing at Louisa's Café, because "truth and art free our souls." *Sunday Ink* opens windows into worlds that I connect to and revel in because these stories are vivid and so well told.

Priscilla Long
Seattle
April 2010

Sandra E. Jones

outhouse

My grandfather and I were reading buddies. He used to bring
home discarded copies of *Reader's Digest* and then, silently, he
and I would spar for private library time in the family outhouse.
Back then, this word-thirsty deacon farmer was fairly well read
given his limited education and we both liked news articles and
the *Reader's Digest*'s pages of quotes and especially the section
called "Life in These United States." He liked to go immediately
after his dawn constitutional. I had to go as soon as I got up.
Sometimes, if it rained, our schedules collided. I always tried
to make sure I got there first. He was sure to be on his way,
if Grandmother didn't delay him with her list of chores and
errands or news about the church community.

A carpenter, whose handsome features would later be compared
to O. J. Simpson's, Granddaddy built every man-made structure
on his property. While he did painting and carpentry work he
would let me tag along, but we never talked about art or color
or design, or concepts. He just created. I chatted and asked
questions and he listened. He cut and I remeasured, holding
the ends of lumber, still warm from the saw, checking to see
if his work turned out as planned. The numbers and fractions
rarely were different from what he'd marked. I remember
wanting him to make a mistake so I would have larger pieces
of scrap lumber to add to my collection of blocks and shapes
for my play housing developments. It seemed he preferred
to demonstrate rather than explain. When we did talk, it
was about things, not people. We didn't talk about anybody
specifically, just the world as a whole, with the exception of
President Eisenhower, whom my grandfather admired and
followed in the two daily newspapers. He liked to catch up on
world news from the outhouse.

From its tiny western window to the spaces between the boards of its door, his hand-hewn toilet was a wonderful place to study sunsets, shadows, and spider webs. It was the perfect place to daydream.

Granddaddy and I worked out a blue theme to accent the whitewashed outhouse. There were two coats of white on the outside but only one very thin tint on its interior walls. He searched the rafters of his backyard smokehouse for unused photos and calendar illustrations, discarding them in order to reuse their frames to display my childhood drawings. He mounted them—complete with a blue background—as the outhouse choice of wall art. Grandmother lent us a cracked blue and white China bowl and pitcher set.

We threw in one of her bleached, feedbag hand towels and the obligatory Sears and Roebuck and Montgomery Ward catalogs she favored. Two pearl-headed stickpins held up the latest Sunday funnies, to which my taciturn Granddaddy was addicted. He built holders near the outhouse floor for magazines. They held *The Tidewater Review, Farmer's Almanac,* community newsletters, and church bulletins. There were also reprints of the ever-present Bible stories. If you didn't stack them in right order, the *Reader's Digest* always slipped through. Ever the considerate designer, he added dowel rests at the bottom of each rack on both walls. This way each user could have handy access to his or her own reading materials.

He designed and built the outdoor toilet as a dual-seater. With a house full of children and the need for accompaniment during late-night trips outdoors, this made sense. To match the toilet's color theme, Grandmother let me use the mesmerizing indigo bluing she saved for special laundry whites. I used it to tint an extra-long dishtowel that we had my grandfather hang freshly starched from the ceiling. He suspended it from a matching blue-wrapped hanger. It served as the sole divider between the two seat holes. That was our decorative attempt at privacy.

Although my grandparents' house had long been equipped with indoor plumbing and electricity, Granddaddy still favored the outhouse. Based on our conversations in the car, that outhouse was a center of reverie and literary transport for both of us. It was where he went to write, to review meeting minutes, and to memorize Bible quotes. Grandmother used to walk down to the outhouse and to the barn to commit poems to memory, practicing aloud, away from the youngest of her eight children. Unless you fell asleep or were extraordinarily inconsiderate, no one dared to interrupt you. Restroom time was sacred time.

I never saw my grandfather or grandmother share that outhouse. Occasionally some guests did, particularly after dark. I later found out how the pairings came about. Most had to do with secrets, death, or borrowed money.

Grandmother used to grumble that Granddaddy and I spent too much time fixing up a place that only required a few minutes' use. She thought our devotion to this project took us away from less-appealing chores.

Neither of us wanted to see her angry nor did we want to hear her nag, so Granddaddy built a flower holder. We took turns filling it. Grandmother was a sucker for flowers—flowers and anything her granddaughter drew. In addition to a clipboard of my garden sketches, we threw in a notepad of jokes and a picture of Jesus Christ. Knowing how important my grandmother's ego was, the young curator in me lettered a label listing her as the generous donor of the items that made using this space important. I got the idea from a class trip to Washington, D.C.

It worked. He and I were over like fat rats. The white toilet with the dual holes, washstand, flowers, and blue accessories was a work of great pride between us.

Later in the summer, I decided to invite Gerald and Lawrence, two neighbor boys from down the road, to check out our cool outhouse. Gerald and Lawrence were my only nearby playmates.

Gerald was a big boy—tall, with dark chocolate skin and large protruding eyes that slanted at the last minute. He had eyelashes so curly they looked like a transparent, striped rug rolled up to his lids. Gerald, three years older but mentally one year younger than I, was born to be led around. Lawrence was like a picture of fruit in a recipe photo, soon to rot despite that hardened lacquer exterior. Lawrence was the tan color of a paper bag and had a long flat head and big, gapped, liar's teeth. At school he was known as Lyin' Larry.

With great young-girl pride, I watched their reaction to our toilet. We took turns peeing and spitting, testing the perfectly cut-out holes, their sound effects and splash acoustics. This mini tour included showing them the four-foot-long spoon my grandfather had fashioned for spreading some kind of bright-yellow lime or sulfur mixture over the solid contents of the dark pit after each use. This giant metal spoon hung from blue string, looped on a nail. Because it was shiny the boys thought it was precious silver. While waiting outside, I heard Larry brag to Gerald that he bet he could get a lot of money for that spoon.

That evening I replaced the blue string with an intricate wire twist and double-nailed it to the wall. I figured Larry would try to steal it one night and I wanted to make this as difficult as possible. From his antics on the school bus and at recess, I figured Lyin' Larry was just as dumb as he was slick. He would never think to just crowbar the nails out of the wall. My grandfather made that spoon too, dammit. Besides the threat of theft, I was annoyed that Larry had caused me to disrupt my color scheme, having to substitute the blue tie for the security of wire. Stupid, Lyin' Larry didn't even have a grandfather or a decent toilet.

That outhouse was associated with lots of memories, where I used to cover both holes with an old tabletop and use it as my clubhouse and play card games with visiting girl classmates, where I would escape into daydreams of fairytales and images of pretty Loretta Young floating down a staircase. It was there that I grew into secretly coveting *forbidden* comic books, where I convened with my dog Skip, my Betsy McCall paper dolls, my doll Laverne, and a reluctant Boots the cat to sort out my childhood affairs.

The only time my grandmother ever beat me, was connected to that toilet. Amazing how central toilets can be to family lore. Once when I was still taking piano lessons, I was going through a very difficult time. I had to live up to my bright, promising student reputation and my fingers and my sense of timing were just not up to it. My concentration was off and I was ashamed. At practice, there was no encouragement, no audience or instructor's feedback.

Worried about piano lessons, acne, hairy legs, I was also in turmoil over Gene Autry Bing and also perplexed by the mysteries of hot ice. I questioned how ice could be hot enough to burn fingers and yet keep ice-cream bars cold at the school's May Day fair. Gene Autry and I had tested it out behind the tent at the Saturday fair. I pondered these issues and whether his offer to be my boyfriend was for real. Gene had complimented me on the downy fuzz on my legs. In return, I admired the rusty fine hairs above his popsicle-reddened lips. Later that day he bought me an orange icicle before he confessed he already had a girlfriend who was really, really pretty. What a miserable afternoon. Besides, the school recital was in less than ten days. In my head, my failure to become a renowned concert pianist would come as a blow to the family. After all they constantly reminded me that they were spending a fortune on my education. Guilt and insecurity trilled the inside of my skull. Puberty was having a befuddling yet empowering effect on me.

Asking my grandmother if I could be excused from my lessons for a restroom break, I stopped practicing Beethoven's *Für Elise* and headed downhill. Sheets of music in hand, I sat down on the lid, panties up and dress down. Copiously scribbling along the white space of the composition, I listed ways to kill myself. Ways so that my death would insure a huge write-up in the news.

I predicted Gene Autry, the snooty girls who excluded me from their group, the boyfriend who had dumped me, and my music teacher would all cry a lot and be sorry I was dead. They would all gather at my grandparents' house and offer their sympathies. I counted on Grandmother to walk them over to the piano and point.

"This is where she died. She practiced herself to death. She wanted, oh, so much, to get this music ready for you but God saw fit to take her instead." My grandmother, the skilled raconteur in the family would paint a very vivid recounting of my short life. Every one of them would cluck their tongues and shake their heads as only people in the country can.

Wh-h-happ! Suddenly the toilet door was flung open with an amazingly inhuman force. My grandmother's arm had become a construction-site jackhammer. I saw the broken switches in her hand.

"Thought you had to go to the bathroom? You were supposed to be done practicing over fifteen minutes ago and here you sit hiding out down here in the outhouse! Get your rump out here right this minute!"

My end-of-life reverie quickly dissipated in the face of her heated anger. She had mistaken my daydreaming for calculated deception.

My grandparents have been dead for decades. Today, the old outhouse, the garage, the barn, pigpen, and chicken coops have long been torn down or just rotted away. The indoor bathroom in their old farmhouse with its aged, light-blue tiles always seemed tired and cold, with never enough room for fantasy.

Carol Bolt

apology to a lobster

The cottage still smells of melted butter and fresh corn. Shells are piled high on the lazy Susan centered on an antique oak table that is creaky from many rowdy meals served there over the years. We'll spend the morning collecting up the evidence of another one of these.

Small round glass bowls with fleshy-pink residue rings and white paper towels crumpled and stained from seafood drippings all are scattered there with no apparent relationship to a "table setting."

We sang to that song from the movie *Carousel* about a real good time. Indeed it was. We knew it would be as we set the table just so. Not too formally as to put off the urges to crush shells, suck the meat from spidery legs, and dunk large chunks of bread into the green tomalley. Lobsterman call this part of the lobster "the brains." It is no wonder we prefer to call it tomalley. The mood could be dampened if we had arranged the table too carefully with fine China and a laced tablecloth. So we rolled out red-and-white checked plastic across the oak table, set places with white clunky cafeteria-style plates, metal tools for cracking and picking, and rolls of paper towels taken directly from the kitchen's counter. These were to wipe clean our chins, hands, and arms. Sometimes "wipe clean" required those green and white little square packets: premoistened towelettes. Needing those is a sign of one's true investment in finding all the best parts of the meal.

As I push the last of a shell pile into a trashbag, the tan plastic bucket nestled in the corner of the room reminds me of an earlier motorboat ride.

You steered the whirring, gurgling motor. I sat with the bucket between my feet, my eyes closed, salt air and spray on my face. The sun was hardly able to keep my hands warm as I clutched the bucket's handle. It's not a long ride across the Sheepscot Bay to Five Islands, but it does require a commitment. We've always allowed two hours. Harbor to wharf is just twenty minutes each way but time is left to dock the boat, walk to the Pound, swap fishing stories with the tending fishermen and, of course, pick just the right specimens for our bucket. We take a few minutes to admire the other boats, the ones we wouldn't mind taking for a spin along the bay. Not a binding contract, which they would otherwise be, but just a quick ride to see if one might be the unforgettable experience that its captain claimed.

Farther up the wharf, we were back to reality. Our fifteen-foot skiff with its peeling paint, 50 horsepower engine, oars included just in case not all 50 horses fire, a scrappy length of rope, a reddish dented gas can, a plastic bottle cut to form a scoop for bailing water, and even the omnipresent quarter-inch of bilge were all a welcomed sight. This was the ride we came for.

With the bucket securely in hand, we set our compass back to the harbor. Perched in the bow I looked down at the sheen of the blackish-red bodies in the worn tan plastic bucket. Their antennae moved side to side. Their compasses set to return to the ocean that skimmed by in short, stiff waves just beneath us. Our focus remained on the orange stick buoy at the mouth of the harbor, where a sentry osprey's nest rests precariously on top. As we slowed to pass the buoy on the starboard side, we were greeted by the peeping of this addition to the harbor family. It is ironic, that Nature has given a grand bird such a hesitant voice.

Safely back in the harbor, you headed the skiff up into the wind. I threw a bowline to catch the cleat on the deck. The plastic on the bucket undulated as the lobsters shifted around inside, adjusting themselves to accommodate an undeserved situation. Under my breath I apologized to them for the way that this was. I thanked them in the next breath for what they were about to sacrifice.

It *was* a real good time. All about our pleasure and their gift.

Pamela Hobart Carter

excerpt from
unhinged

CHARACTERS
LYLE GREEN—tweedy university professor, 60ish
CAITLIN BOWER GREEN—his wife, 60ish
CHARLES GARDNER—neighbor of CAITLIN and LYLE, 50ish
SALLY TANNER—a judge, 40
A WAITER

TIME
Early 21st century.

SETTINGS
*GREENS's kitchen with two exits, one to the hall, one to the garden—including
a big tree; bedroom—doubles as GREENS's and SALLY's; a café.*

ACT I

SCENE—May (in progress)

SALLY, LYLE, and CHARLES sit at a café table.

SALLY
Everyone encourages. Everyone asks all the others at least one
question. Everyone listens.

LYLE
This is not your courtroom.

CAITLIN returns, sits.

SALLY
Everywhere I go is my courtroom, especially where you're
concerned.

CAITLIN
Sally's like you, Lyle. Everywhere you go is your classroom.

SALLY
What do you do, Charles?

CHARLES
Bake cookies, lie on my back, look at the sky.

LYLE
Perhaps Sally meant, to make a living?

CHARLES
This is how I make a life. How about you, Sally?

SALLY
Do you know what Charles does?

CAITLIN
Fixes broken things.

SALLY
Lyle, are you a handyman?

WAITER
(Arrives with tray of food, consults notes, he lays down in front of SALLY)
"The Full Caesar, no anchovies," *(in front of LYLE)* "One
snapper, cloaked in pepper sauce," *(in front of CHARLES)* "Sole
on a bed of earth greens and root vegetables," *(and in front of
CAITLIN)* "Today's fresh catch." Forgive the chef's pun, the
Carp Diem.

SCENE—June

Afternoon. CAITLIN and SALLY sit at same café. CAITLIN sketches SALLY. SALLY reads happily.

CAITLIN
It was time to draw you. I'll post you on the wall on my side of the bed so I see you when I wake up in the morning.

SALLY
Please, don't put me in your bedroom.

CAITLIN
You have your clothes on, Sally!

SALLY
It's as if I'm a third wheel, or watching.

CAITLIN
(Smiling.) I can turn the drawing to the wall at certain times.

SALLY
Ugh. You're not making things better. Put me somewhere else, Caity. Put me in the bathroom.

CAITLIN
I could make you portable like those shrines we saw at the Asian Art Museum.

SALLY
A portable shrine, then. Am I a deity now, Cait? You make too much of me.

CAITLIN
It's not too much to recognize you.

SALLY
You haven't eaten that sandwich.

CAITLIN
I've decided to eat only when I'm really hungry.

SALLY
What does Lyle do?

CAITLIN
Scorns me. Laughs.

SALLY
I mean about meals? Isn't he the three-square type?

CAITLIN
He hasn't been around much at dinner. This conference has him so busy.

SALLY
I thought the conference was last week?

CAITLIN
For the public. These academics stick together for another week doing who knows what.

SALLY
Yes, who knows? Did you meet Sabina Ruiz?

CAITLIN
She actually admired my cloud paintings. A friend of hers has a gallery. Sabina took pictures with her cell phone to show her and her friend said I should make more for an exhibition, in a couple of months.

SALLY
Caitlin! A show! I would have led with that.

CAITLIN
I've decided to take the door off.

SALLY
Let's take all the doors off! *(Pause.)* What do you mean?

CAITLIN
Do away with the kitchen door.

SALLY
No door?

CAITLIN
No door. Be able to be in my kitchen and my garden at the same time.

SALLY
Um. How do you think Lyle will like that?

CAITLIN
You're very worried about Lyle. He probably won't notice for a week or two.

SALLY
I think he'll notice a door missing.

CAITLIN
He's oddly unresponsive to his environment. He never climbs trees.

SALLY
I don't climb trees.

CAITLIN
That's a shame. Changes your point of view. It would probably alter your judgments in the courtroom. It's almost as good as

being on the water for bringing me to peace. I learn birdsongs. This is the finch.

SALLY
I know the fucking robin at four in the morning. I think about a gun.

CAITLIN
You're a hyperbolist!

SALLY
How's it coming? I have a hearing at two.

CAITLIN
I always wondered what judges did with their super-long lunch breaks. Now I know they're sitting for their portraits.

SALLY
Aren't you worried about thieves? Raccoons? Weather?

CAITLIN
It's not forever.

SALLY
Can't you just leave the door open when you're around? I'd worry about my camera, my TV, my self—

CAITLIN
I think people will be respectful, or they can have the stuff. I haven't watched TV since I was laid off. They can have the TV.

SALLY
But strangers walking in—what if Lyle wants to watch something? What if—

CAITLIN
Stop worrying. Enjoy your book. Lyle doesn't watch TV much anyway.

SALLY
It's a little weird, Honey.

CAITLIN
I've decided not to concern myself with weird by not thinking about judgment at all. I am simply doing. Making. Thanking you for saving my life by using it every day.

ACT II

SCENE—June

In the garden, CHARLES and CAITLIN paint. The door is gone.

CHARLES
You're like one of those grubs.

CAITLIN
I beg your pardon?

CHARLES
You're coming out of the ground—leaving the Archives—surfacing, as if you're a different creature. You know how people used to believe in spontaneous generation? It was because they didn't observe closely enough to see metamorphosis. The creature that emerges from the grub has the same DNA. All this creativity has been in you. You're the same person, and not. You're manifesting yourself newly.

CAITLIN
So what does that make me?

CHARLES
A beetle.

They laugh.

CAITLIN
OK, sharing time! *(They spin their paintings so the other can see.)*
Charles, I'm—I look very happy. A little orange. But happy.

CHARLES
That was the intention.

CAITLIN
It's just, what are you doing?
I thought this whole
time here . . . was different.
Was about something else.

CHARLES
I didn't want to paint
a landscape.

CHARLES
It was about those things and this too. We'd better get these in.
That was a raindrop.

Run into the kitchen with the wet paintings—prop them on chairs, etc.

CHARLES
I'll change and be right back. *(Exits.)*

CAITLIN sits and begins writing, no stops. LYLE enters from hall, walks straight to doorway. CAITLIN keeps writing through this scene.

LYLE
Caitlin, what happened? Did someone break our door?

CAITLIN
Took it clean off the hinges.

LYLE
The door is gone?

CAITLIN
I like the access. Walk through it a few times. You'll see
what I mean.

LYLE
What did the police say?

CAITLIN
Why would I bother them?

LYLE
Maybe they can find our door. Was anything else taken?

CAITLIN
No. We could do with fewer material goods anyway. You're always telling me that.

LYLE
Caitlin, this is not what I meant. I want to select.

CAITLIN
But you never do. Why not let someone else? Besides, we're both so busy.

LYLE
You plan to leave it like this?

CAITLIN
It's pleasant in the kitchen. I'll get you an iced tea. Just sit, Lyle. Tomorrow, I'm going to spend the whole day sitting, I think. Maybe on our grass.

LYLE
Caity, I think you should see a doctor.

CAITLIN
Because I want to sit on the grass?

LYLE
This is too much.

CAITLIN
You care that much about the toaster? Do you care about this chair? Is your heart in this chair? Let the chair go, Lyle. *(Looks up.)* What's crazy is never questioning convention, being little lambs trotting after the shepherd—only you can't name why. You can only "Baaaa."

CAITLIN pours two glasses of iced tea and sets them near a vase of flowers. The table is crowded with art projects. Cloud paintings on all the walls. LYLE pauses, sits, drinks. CAITLIN sits, drinks, takes his hand, smiles. He does not.

CAITLIN
It's all right, Lyle. Everything is all right.

Long beat.

LYLE
What are we eating tonight?

CAITLIN
I don't know. I was—busy. Let's go out. We could introduce Charles to one of the local joints.

LYLE
That would be nice of us.

CAITLIN
Or get some takeout?

LYLE
I am famished. I am fatigued. The door is missing. I return home to find you scribbling and no hint of dinner anywhere. Did you call someone to replace the door? What are you doing?

CAITLIN
Writing a great American novel. Is there something wrong with that?

LYLE
If it precludes eating. And buying food. And cooking. And our
dinner. And a door to shut.

CHARLES knocks on doorframe.

LYLE
To wit. The thug from next door is here.

CAITLIN
Oh, I invited Charles to dinner.

LYLE
What dinner?

CAITLIN
Hello.

CHARLES
Hello. May I come in? Oh, Caitlin! *(About a painting.)*
It's perfect!

CAITLIN
Thank you.

CHARLES and CAITLIN sit after she pours him iced tea.

CAITLIN
I'm so wrapped up in my novel. I was kind of still there.

CHARLES
Sounds like a good book. What are you reading?

CAITLIN
Writing.

CHARLES
Is there anything you don't do?

LYLE
Prepare dinner!

CHARLES
I've always wanted to live next door to a writer. What's it about?

CAITLIN
Oh, thank you for asking. Teenagers.

CHARLES
Why teenagers?

CAITLIN
It's how the story came to me.

CHARLES
It just showed up in your head?

CAITLIN
I woke with it there one morning. *(Indicates spot on head.)*

LYLE
Do adults want to read about teenagers?

CHARLES
Remember how horrible the cafeteria was?

CAITLIN
A very raw place. For the teachers too. I don't want the teacher
to be a creep. He's fresh out of college—only five or six years
between them.

LYLE
He has affairs with them?

CHARLES
It will be hard to make him likable then.

LYLE
Maybe he possesses a sense of humor or the student instigates.

CAITLIN
Why would she?

CHARLES
She thinks he's handsome . . .

LYLE
 . . . a better grade . . .

CHARLES
 . . . experience . . .

LYLE
 . . . horniness, to revenge her beau. Adventure.

CAITLIN
I want them to be friends. The girl and the teacher—and
everyone thinks there's something going on that shouldn't be,
but there's not, really. Only they're not really allowed to be
friends because it engenders suspicion. So even the friendship
is taboo. And then he thinks, if everyone already thinks we're
involved, why don't we—but, then he realizes that he really loves
her and he won't do anything that could hurt her heart, not
talking about her reputation here, he's thinking about what
matters. And he doesn't want to jeopardize the friendship.

LYLE
I would read it if there were some good sex scenes.

CHARLES
A friendship story is hard to find.

Arleen Williams

letting go

It was early dawn and already the Mexico City airport was crowded. My youngest sister, Maureen, was leaving after a two-week visit. For me, it was a joyous time getting to know a sister six years younger, a sister barely into the double digits when I left home at seventeen. Now I lived in Mexico City, married to a Mexican national. Maureen was finishing her degree at a community college near Seattle, Washington. The youngest of nine siblings, she struggled to find herself and her place in the world.

We had spent the evening before with calendar in hand, planning her next visit. I convinced her that she could stay for as long as she wanted. I was desperate for the family that I felt had long forgotten me. Maureen's visit was unique, and I didn't want it to end.

At the airport that morning it was my husband who thought of the camera. *"Dejame sacar una foto,"* he said. I hate having my photograph taken, but that day I didn't resist. Maureen and I wrapped ourselves in a tangle of arms and smiles and laughter. I thought little of the photograph at the time.

The flight was called. We gave each other one last tight hug. I kissed her on both cheeks and promised to write. She assured me she would be back the following summer for a much longer visit. She would work extra hours, save as much as possible, and buy an open-ended ticket. I took comfort in that promise.

She walked through the gate toward the plane, turning only once to give a quick little backward wave over her right shoulder. Tears tracked my cheeks as I returned the gesture. Her plane pulled from the gate and taxied down the tarmac. I stood and watched small specks crisscrossing the sky, unsure which plane was hers, but unwilling to walk away. After a time, my husband guided me to our battered green VW bug. I cried as we drove through the busy streets of early morning Mexico. The crowds of pedestrians, the honking, the cursing, the smog could not stop the sharp pain stabbing my heart.

Was it premonition? Was my body aware of a truth that my mind could not yet know? Is that why I held Maureen so close, feeling her heart beating against my own as my husband took that last photograph? That photograph of two sisters at the Mexico City airport is all I have left of my baby sister. She was murdered a year after Mexicana Airlines carried her home to Seattle. To this day, I wish I had never let go.

Carol Bolt

the gift

It turns out I didn't know the meaning of a gift at all prior
to 1975. It was then, at 12 years old, in Cozy Harbor, Maine,
I began to understand.

The gift arrived on a trailer pulled by a bubble-fendered,
1957 Chevy pickup. Truck and trailer were almost as loosely
put together as the little boat itself. All three creaked, groaned,
and made grinding noises as their combined efforts backed
the truck's trailer into a grassy spot next to the cottage. As
the chunky wooden hull brushed by, the adjacent rocky herb
garden released clouds of fragrance: dill, lavender, and mint.
The little Turnabout sailboat had been set in its spot.

To give you an idea of what we were dealing with—a sail number
coincides with the age of a boat. The lower the number
the older the boat. That year's molded fiberglass fleet was
numbered in the latter two thousands. Turnabouts hadn't been
made out of wood since the editions numbered in the eight
hundreds. This boat's number was 270.

My father took measurements and absorbed my mother's
directives. She had quickly summed up the situation, made a
package and wrapped it, "Let's paint it grey, black, orange, and
white and call it *Puffin*!" she said.

The only question she posed was, "Just *how* is all this work going
to get done?"

With that still in the air and no definitive duty roster assigned,
Dad and I were off to gather supplies. The work would get done
in a centuries-old-art-world kind of way; Dad as the Patron
and me the starry-eyed worker bee. I could not have been more

excited. This was a project with a functioning sum, complete with power tools and cool colors. I was giddy. Some of the changes would be purely cosmetic but most would be necessary to keep what remained of the sailboat's disintegrating wooden hull in the shape of a seaworthy vessel. The adventure had officially begun.

So Dad and I, each with a hamburger in hand—from the parking lot's lunch counter that was really just a toolshed with an open window—began scouting the aisles of that shoppe as we would for many seasons to come. We read a lot of labels but mostly quizzed the shoppe-keepers: What would this paint do that that one couldn't? What exactly *is* dry rot and can it be fixed? Each recurring summer would begin with the same inquiry: "Which *new & improved* sealant would keep the bay in the bay?"

The water that this ten foot vessel took on during the six years that I sailed it served as a significant mentor. A little in, a little out, keep the cycle going around. My top mission was to keep the sail full of wind and us both moving forward. It seemed to me, the more consistently we moved the less water I took on. Stuckness was not an option for as long as whatever my 12-year-old mind had defined as "success" continued to be the goal of the journey.

Many dollars later, with brushes, paint, tapes, sealant, scrapers, rags, sandpaper, a variety of boat builders' remedies in hand and their stories in mind, we returned from our first visit to Brewer's Marine & Hardware store. I set to work. It took weeks of scraping, sanding, patching, painting, scraping, sanding, more patching, and more painting—and plenty of waiting and removing splinters in between. The summer sun was as hot and satisfying as the transformation. My nose was full with those aromatic herbs, my eyes challenged by the harbor's anticipating saltwater, and my ears entertained with Casey

Kasem's jockeying of music industry anecdotes on my red plastic transistor radio. All of these served as a supportive team. I sang and scraped to Joni Mitchell, *Sweet Baby James*, and Simon & Garfunkel.

Only a couple of weeks remained of summer when the last of the patches was sealed, the paint cured, and the sail's hardware installed. Soon I would get to introduce *Puffin* into Cozy Harbor's corps. This would be the test of not only my handy skills and my sailing skills but also of my preteen esteem. Once it's on the water, a boat's success would be obvious and well witnessed. The soundness and aesthetic of a boat's restoration is of considerable note in an intimate New England waterfront town, especially in a competitive summer community. It would be difficult to make light of or for that matter sail an ailing craft. I wouldn't know for sure until it had been set afloat and enough time passed to see if the hull would swell in correct proportion to keep up with the persistent pressure of the ocean. There are good reasons why they mold boats in fiberglass—lack of seams would place high on that list. Now, I think that life is probably much too short to own and actually sail a wooden boat, but at the time, the difficulties couldn't dissuade a naïve yet determined, budding sailor.

On a cool marine fragrant morning in August 1975, the gift *Puffin* slid over popping seaweed and gooey mudflats to be received by a choir of cackling gulls and a cheer from friends and family.

I have received many generous, loving gifts in the years since the *Puffin* for which I am grateful, but truthfully none has called for such considered attention, shaped me so markedly, or been such a perfect fit.

Sandra E. Jones

sleeping in

The expression "sleep in" wasn't one heard around the Lower East Side. One usually just slept late or slept all morning. This often prompted the questions, "Are you going to sleep all day? Planning to get up any time soon?" But not, "Do you plan to sleep in?"

"Sleeping in? Sleeping in what?" would be most people's boomerang response. The Italians, Jews, Poles, and Ukrainians living within the L-shaped boundary of New York's Houston Street and the East River didn't have time in their industrious lives for sleeping in. But Taras Nickolai Gogol did. Mr. Taras Gogol slept in. Literally and consistently.

Hattie Roanoke and Taras Gogol lived in the same building. Gogol and Hattie had known each other since 1967, when they both moved in on the same September weekend. Highly organized Hattie had reserved the freight elevator, the preoccupied Mr. Gogol hadn't.

Twenty-five years later, Hattie began a new line of work in assisted-living. She was also the liaison who coordinated medical, housing, and transport issues and Mr. Gogol was one of her clients. She usually saw Mr. Gogol once a week.

Hattie sat with her daughter Corrine on the generous concrete balcony looking out over the Columbus Street area high rises. Corrine was born during Hattie's marriage to a North African vendor whose mother commandeered a major portion of her late son's life and the lives of his offspring too. The woman hadn't approved of her granddaughter being raised in the United States or her dual citizenship status. Corrine grew up with her father's family and came stateside for visits. With

the deaths of Corrine's father and grandmother, Hattie and her daughter had been reunited for nearly three years before Corrine returned to Africa to get married.

At noon they were joined by Yolanda Blake, an old family friend from the '70s. Yolanda was visiting from San Diego. Corrine looked at her mother and then turned to look at Yolanda. Surprisingly, her mother appeared more youthful. Both women were attractive but in different packaging. Yolanda was rail-thin and wore a lot of makeup. She also wore a cheerful, witty cover over deeply embedded sarcasm. Hattie was a full-bodied size fourteen and rarely attempted any serious measures to be glamorous beyond mascara.

Corrine had come to assess the fee-controlled condo and to see her mother's much-talked-about friend Yolanda. Eagle-eyed Aunt Joan wasn't part of the financial plan. Early on, Corrine's mother had bought into the building and renovated a few things but not enough to match the new flavor of zigzagging condos nearby. Still, it was prime, prime real estate.

Corrine had found her Aunt Joan's friend, Yolanda, interesting and decided to stay past lunch to get Yolanda's take on all things New York, especially the past, the part that seemed to bore Hattie when she asked her mother for details.

It seemed Hattie was now the 17th floor's only holdout. Most of the building's population was made up of second-generation flight attendants who inherited units stocked with new faces as roommates.

At the beginning of the disco age, way before Corrine was even a thought, Hattie had been a Pan Am flight attendant. Back then she flew under the more exotic name, Hata. Her sister Joan and Joan's pal Yolanda used to party in New York. The

two younger women would come over from New Jersey to use Hattie's often vacated place as their launching pad, where they parked New Jersey boys and took New York guys for a spin.

In the summer of '71 Hata took a long-term assignment in Italy and the girls made good on that streak of uninterrupted freedom during her overseas stay. Joan and Yolanda hadn't dared to blow the luxury of access to Hattie's lower Manhattan digs. The building was filled with Pan Am, TWA, SAS and other airline people who knew Hattie. People with irregular work and sleep schedules.

The girls had had little opportunity to meet many of the neighbors, but four or five faces and names still stuck with them. Two handsome male flight attendants at the other end of the hall who started including them in a couple of inner circle parties, the middle-aged couple, the Markowitzes, and Mr. Gogol, the man downstairs who always donned one of several interesting jackets whenever he came up to say hello.

As the three women reminisced, the events and exchanges came back. Corrine listened to past stories centered around this high rise. It seemed that her mother and aunt had charmed or befriended the gays and the old people and ignored all the loud Texan pilots and Nordic model types.

Yolanda threw out another blast from the past, "And the older guy with the cool tweed jackets trimmed in velvet and suede. What's the deal with him? He was always hitting on you Joan."

The balcony door slid open and Joan's doelike face appeared. She stepped out on the balcony and dropped her bags and grabbed each woman for a hug. Joan, the athlete, wore a chic but simple shirt over leggings and expensive sandals. Her face was a fairly good copy of her sister Hattie's. Joan and Yolanda were due for a quick weekend reunion and Joan hadn't seen

Hattie since the three weeks they'd spent in Philadelphia following their dad's death in April. Getting their parents' row house cleaned out—removing all the suits, ties, and train collections of their railroad-loving dad—had taken up most of the rest of the month. She checked out her niece Corrine who hadn't made it to the funeral and had spent this last week paying her respects to select members of the family.

"Give Aunt Joanie some sugar." Her niece's hug was loose and tepid. Corrine was grown up and now lived in Morocco with a family of her own. A small residue of distance in her demeanor mirrored the miles on her passport. "Now who was this who was always hitting on me?"

"Oh, come on, Joan, you remember the man who was insulted because we thought he was Jewish? Mr. Gogol. Down in 1611."

"He was the one who would always leave roses on Valentine's Day and at Thanksgiving." Yolanda's pictures of Mr. Taras Gogol began redeveloping in her mind's eye. She had liked Mr. T.—her name for the quiet but suave man who was always writing. She had gone down to his place to return a check and a ten-dollar bill stuck in the back of a magazine they'd borrowed from him while chatting on the way up from the mailboxes. He was sworn to them forever after. She noticed a couple of busy-looking typewriters and lots of clean piles of books and paper.

"Not the cool older guy? Dang! I had forgotten about him. Is he still alive?"

Yes, Mr. T. was still alive. Taras Gogol—a Ukrainian immigrant who didn't seem to work outside the home was alive and well. It had become clear over the years that he was never quite as old as they originally thought. Hattie explained that he was now one of her clients, now that she no longer worked for the airlines. From the looks of most of his paperwork he was only 69 years old.

"You know he sleeps in a vulva."

In the stillness after that statement, they could hear the East River winds whipping by the balcony.

"He what?" asked Corrine, looking at her mother suspiciously. This was not information she thought a mother should know about a man she wasn't married to and Corrine thought it even a less appropriate revelation to make.

"Mr. Gogol, that's right, Taras, sleeps in a vulva."

"Oh, Hat you can't be serious!" said Joan, reverting back to her old name for big sister Hattie.

"And how would you know?" questioned a stunned but piqued Yolanda.

"Well, let's just say I had occasion to visit him. You all remember how the place was covered with stacks and stacks of newspapers going back to near the turn of the century. *New York Times* were everywhere—magazines, labels on various subject matter and reference materials—were everywhere one looked. There were literally paths to his front door, kitchen, and bathroom. The city was called in for code violations and as part of the building committee we eventually gained access. A couple of us who knew him over the years helped him beat back City Hall and paperwork. He agreed to supervised housecleaning and some de-cluttering. As he got older he depended less and less on places like the Katz Deli and Gertle's Bakery and other takeout standbys. He took a few cooking lessons from Danny Gye who lost his partner Teddy—you know the party guys who lived across from the loose Barbies? The loose Barbies worked for SAS and did the three-ways. Remember? Anyway . . ."

"Never mind the cooking. What about the woman's parts? We aren't talking John Wayne Gacy or Jeffrey Dahmer scenes

are we?" Yolanda zoomed in for the 411.

"No, Yo, nothing like that." Hattie calmly explained, "This is a bed, a specially made bed. It appears to be carved out of some therapeutic, shape-to-your-form kind of mattress foam material. At first I thought it was a skinny Valentine with pages but Mr. Gogol set me straight."

Corrine gave a straight-out-of-Jane-Austen sniff and turned her huge, proud, half African head to the south as if Chinatown were a new cologne wafting her way. Hattie's daughter was clearly uncomfortable with the visuals.

Joan thought it was funny, but was more intrigued by the humorous effect than the details. She wondered who made it for him? What color was it? Was it real-like or blue and orange or plaid like a flannel wrap? Was it some sort of snuggly gone bad?

Hattie put them out of some of their misery. "It's covered in various flesh-colored fabrics, shaped and textured to resemble a woman's parts. It's not exactly heart-shaped but it's wider at the head than it is at the foot. What am I doing explaining the shape to you guys? Not a soul out here on this patio is without one and even if you aren't using it, you all still have mirrors."

Yolanda thought about it for a while and began to chuckle. It had been ages since she'd seen hers. The last decade, whether her husband was home or not, she just showered, dried off and quickly dressed. Except for a few obligatory breast exams every quarter, Yolanda's bathroom mirror was restricted to a neck-up tilt, for flossing and brushing and mascara positions only. She began to laugh. A tiny little giggle at first, then laughter ran out of her faster than menopausal pee.

They all cracked up. There were starts and snorts and then

more bursts of laughter. Except for Corrine, but even she couldn't repress a smile.

A vulva? Why didn't he just burrow himself into a sleeping bag? Was the opening on his mattress a simple slit, a hole, a normal twin-size body space? Surely that must be what it looked like. Her mom must be mistaken. Without realizing it, Corrine sat there shaking her head.

"Hattie, you have to tell us what did it feel like? Did you touch it? What did he say when he knew you had seen it? And by the way, how did you get to see his bedroom?" Yolanda and Joan had the same questions.

They drew a collective groan once everyone thought about the ramifications.

"Well, as it did turn out he did do some work for the *Times*. He had something on somebody it seems. Besides being a ghost writer, he wrote for and produced occasional porn scripts and magazines. He said there was not much to them. So for a few inane lines, some grunting and screaming, 'Oh, baby, oh, baby,' he made a fortune. He hid money in the stacks of newsprint, books, and other printed materials but his deceased wife's stepson came to America and sought him out and eventually talked his way in and ripped him off. He didn't get everything, but enough to make a dent."

"Yeah, I'd say he left a dent." No one expected a wiseacre quip from Corrine.

"Nice one," smiled Yolanda. "I would pay money to see that." Yolanda was thinking photos.

"Me too," said Joan.

Hattie brought the group up to speed with this history of Taras Gogol. "I was there to review his meds with him. He was short of breath so I followed him into the bedroom to help him look for his tray of prescriptions and OTC treatments. That's when I noticed it. I almost sat on it. It is part pink, part dried peach, part apricot, and it faced a corner. It reminds me of an art installation, an ode to Philip Johnson and outsider quilt artists. One side was a couple of slivers of pale velvet against deep brownish and ruddy-colored fabric. It's like it belongs to an Asian, Hispanic, and African blend of a woman's anatomy. It's all rich brocades, lush velvets, chenille, and silk and has pale almost rose-shaped bumps in strategic places. The room was clean and neat except for dust on the upper blinds and windowsill. It smelled of Downy or some kind of clean laundry fragrance. It would appear that he crawls into what looks like a satin and fleece-lined body bag and then slides down into the vaginal opening."

No one said a word. Corrine was surprised at her mother's almost clinical detachment about this bizarre room downstairs. Joan and Yolanda hadn't remembered Hattie's interest in anything remotely aesthetic, and here she was sounding like their old art history days.

The four women took up various relaxed sitting and standing postures on the New York City balcony. Joan laid out croissants and spreads for all. They nibbled the expensive snacks while in the August distance, the Williamsburg Bridge looked tired and not nearly as inspiring as it had on those dreamy nights in the '70s.

Geri Gale

zero through nine

I love the horror of zero
dressing up in obscurity
the unknown snuff of the candle
call me stranger geranium.

I ride Otis to the most-elevated floor
dance the tango, the fox trot, the cha-cha-
cha, with friends among the dead and unborn—
so many living disappoint me.

I unravel the clutch you have on me
the promiscuous persimmon of strait intimacy
your tempest shipwrecked hold on me
"Yes," the siren answered. "They call it love."

I take all the necessary
(horrible and very lovely) steps,
pass white-picket fences
pass car-spitting pistons
past girdled grace and windless steadfast.

In the small of my back
a hand heats my oven
desert-city blood loosens
my jew-jew laughter
am I a stranger on a train?

This spring changes climate
unmanned by her as well
bride-to-bride altars——
bye-bye to murdering men
sewing quilts of female skin.

This make-everything-clear-and-easy era,
history, a nightmare I try to awake from
my freedom hinges
upon the last king being strangled
with the entrails of the last priest.

For this is my body
sweet body secret sixteen.
For this is the golden girl
shrilling settling seething
in the wild wild west.
For this is my brain, my shame, my fame
for this is my gem, my hem, my r.e.m.
for this is my time our time in time
to join my body rune-rime.

But how was I to know all this?
The famished usurper knocked on my door
seduced me with gifts and riches
crawled and roped underneath my skin
robed me ugly and without.

So now, with needle and thread
and metal mast white sail love
I, the horrible and very lovely,
red-orange geranium,
bloom-burst through the coursed
all-too-human cursed wind.

Geri Gale

her disappearance

pittore/pennello

A crisp air from outside
sweeps across her sleeping-beauty face
an opium of restraint
a muted tinge of laughter
mutters through slight parted lips
she is the child once again
that he paints into the bark of his/her existence
an eternal blessed silence of knowledge and retribution,
for revenge sways
a flag of surrender
to the whims of playfulness.

Toward the testicle of time
Leonardo punishes himself
for his desire to kiss and wake her from sleep
for his hold of her leather reins
to ride with her in the conversation
divine, fountain of youth
waterfalls of spouted truth,
neither rain nor pour
but a modest hemispheric fall
of liquid seething from stone lips
unearthing the refusal
his blasphemous denial:
I take from her to please myself.

dipinto

In the balconies of the lady
in the eyes and in the mouth
vulnerabilities to change
stolen sentiments of remorse
the heroine of the misplaced
in the castle, in the private/public chamber
women and men to sea, each waiting, in line
to witness, to steal, to heal
the graven image behind Plexiglas
her black corset chest rises and trembles
killings of nations
of kings and queens
and dominions and dynasties of confession.
The keepers, the sleepers do not tend
or perhaps alchemy in the pigments
Leonardo ground
to disappear
at the appropriate hour
of death, no traveler returns.

And then, he pulls one loose thread
a secretive tug
not even the pigeons can hear
and he circle-swipes shadows around her neck
as if wearing a ruthless black tree, all the while
she slumbers and pretends to worship Him.

Leonardo drops the paintbrush to the floor.
"Why stop?" she asks like a child.
"No paint will paint what I see today."
"I am tired of waiting," she lifts her hands
right hand atop left hand to waist,
"Paint my injury today."

He bends to the floor
rehands his wood
a ceremony he performs on Friday
when bored. He sucks the spicy-salty
Mediterranean caper
he carries as a mouth-charm.
Our Lady of Sorrows,
leaves him at the appropriate hour
of death, no traveler returns.

Geri Gale

the portrait of a cold tear

Men like that. Love among the tombstones. Romeo. Spice of pleasure.
In the midst of death we are in life. Both ends meet.

It possessed him.
The cold tear cleft to her cheek.
If he could step up close to touch it
he knew it would bite his flesh.
The way with tears.
With coulds and wounds.
But he preferred to remain at a distance.

Men like that. Love among the tombstones. Romeo. Spice of pleasure.
In the midst of death we are in life. Both ends meet.

Her hands interlaced
fingers bloodred in the sittingroom.
One red velvet couch, one leather chair, one stone fireplace.
She watched the flames
admired the burning wood with eyes
of a woman who loved an artist.
When she posed for the painter, rosehands
full of blood.

Men like that. Love among the tombstones. Romeo. Spice of pleasure.
In the midst of death we are in life. Both ends meet.

Possession ate at him
wind pounded the window,
tugged his hand to continue with black.
Brutality black.
Murderous. Bleeding. Black. Desire.
He was one of them.
He had his paints and he had his time.
He fathered the bloom of a wandering jewel.

Men like that. Love among the tombstones. Romeo. Spice of pleasure.
In the midst of death we are in life. Both ends meet.

One.
She gave him one.
She taunted with one.
She harbored the others for herself.
She was rich in tears
a flooded delta
trees rooting earth.
The painter likened it to Romeo.
The secret dust the poet kept to himself.
You must distance yourself.
They devour your heart.

Men like that. Love among the tombstones. Romeo. Spice of pleasure.
In the midst of death we are in life. Both ends meet.

The painting, the sad lonely painting
one day may hang on a rich man's wall.
The sad lonely painting nailed on the wall
dusted with a whitecloth.
The cold tear cleft to the woman's cheek.
Her lace collar scratched her skin.
When the painter had painted the detail of lace
he had felt the scratch of her skin.

Men like that. Love among the tombstones. Romeo. Spice of pleasure.
In the midst of death we are in life. Both ends meet.

The perfect angle of the paintbrush
erased a shadow
unveiled pure white.
Other artists kill themselves
to unearth her pure white.
Nadja played the violin
wore pants,
they said her body moved too much.
She tried to kill herself
but the pistol jammed.

Men like that. Love among the tombstones. Romeo. Spice of pleasure.
In the midst of death we are in life. Both ends meet.

And so the painter left black,
returned to red,
to the sweet, sickly scent of blood,
safe red,
homegrown red,
hemorrhaged red.

It possessed him.
A rich fragile world possessed him
an artful world, not a soul's breath heard.

Geri Gale

eaten

She stands buried
in thought
cumbrous flesh
curves of her body, black lines
waiting to be colored
purple-brown   Gauguin toes
voluptuous-green   Frida hips
          amazon bones.
Small steps.
Married to her feet
she counts her toes.
A deep-belly pulse
she moves slow.
Pectoral, abdominal, dorsal
muscles squeeze
heirloom thighs inner spiral
shins thrust forward
calves reverse backward
folds of her lips divide
          body inside out.
Shoulder blades slip into back ribs
plates of land shift underneath
arteries pump   two wings at her chest
back bends   heart softens
rebellious hands   limber fingers
          arms spill blood.
She is a young girl again
unafraid to fall
poised to fly
she can soar to the sun
and her wings will not melt.

Landscape-lover
ears a tunnel of consumption
basket of loneliness
braided river blood
men pass,
one two three four
winter spring summer fall
love that dare not speak its name
          she ferries herself across alone.

New York City skating on ice
Tucson sinking in sand
her sacrum bedded in France
a sliver of her heart in Israel
          she is no longer an individual.
She stretches
one vertebra at a time
twenty-six bones
fire in bones
heat through wound
a vessel churning
the press of human being
worn-torn   purple-brown   Gauguin toes
pilfered   voluptuous-green   Frida hips.
Bones turn to wax
liquid melts and drips
one tear unfolds
sidles between breasts
to the dark navel well
tear after tear
          molten lava.
She opens her lips
receives a million seeds
she chooses only one.

Eaten and spewed
on a bed of green moss
a mound of red volcanic ash
a part of western civilization
she counts
five thousand
seven hundred
sixty-four
        years of betrayal. Exiled
at age seventy-seven
she suffocates, her mouth
with a plastic bag.

Geri Gale

schema

SCENE: a green leaf careens a concrete crevice, coalesces constraint & continuance

ORGAN: elysian eyes envision essential evolution & ecstasy, easy elusive effervescence

ART: poetess pummels palpitations & prolific periods & permanent parallels & pleading pomegranates

COLOR: cerulean conversations convince & convolute clouds & coronas & corollas

SYMBOL: surrogate sexual slips & skips swerves sways swoons succulent singular sonnets & serum

TECHNIQUE: hardness hones hellish haloes & horrific honeymoons & hollowed holiness

CORRESPONDENCE: dialogue deems dogged delirium & delicious daunting doomed dates & dumb-de-dum diaphragms donned done

PERSONS: clandestine clans clamor chance confluence & cohabitation comeliness

SENSE: meaning measures magnitudes & mirth & malice & moistens mundane moments, moored mystery a green leaf

Arleen Williams

writing at louisa's

The room hums with creative energy as I rush into Louisa's
Café & Bakery five minutes late. Diners sit chattering at the
scattered tables along the outer walls of the room, the hum of
music barely audible over clattering of pots and pans from the
open kitchen. But as I join the group of writers at the center
tables, it is not those sounds I hear. As I sit and open my own
notebook, I tune inward listening for my inner voice. Instead
I feel the whispers of other voices. The voices of my fellow
writers, the voices of their characters fill the air, their stories
surging from head to hand, from pen to paper.

We gather twice a week, year after year, to bleed our stories, ink
onto paper. We write and share these stories, knowing we are
supported and nourished by the experience. The timer is set
at two-thirty and sounds at three o'clock. For thirty minutes
stories float through the air and find rest on blank pages.
Stories that must be told because silence kills, because truth
and art free our souls.

We are a fluid mix of Seattle writers, young and old, female and
male, experienced and first-timers, published and still-to-be.
What we share is the desire to find voice and to express our
soul in words. We play with language to record or create lives
and worlds that prior to that moment when pen grazes paper
live only in the diverse worlds of our individual memories or
imaginations. We come to Louisa's, we scribble our stories, real
and imagined, and we breathe life into them.

When the timer jolts us back to present time, we share the
words we have written, each voice unique—some soft, smooth,
and soothing, others deep, rough, or halting. We laugh, we cry,
we get embarrassed, and we find the support we need to pull

us back each week to scribble more words in what seem at times to be nothing more than illegible ink stains. We return each week not for any illusions of notoriety, not even for the dream of publication, but simply because the voices inside our heads will not be silenced in any other manner. Those voices demand to be heard, so we come together and give them life—our stories intertwined in the gentle scratches of pen on paper at Louisa's Café & Bakery.

the disorder

My recital was coming up and getting ready took all my effort. This morning I put coffee on the stove, then went straight to the violin. I began with slow scales, stretched-out sounds that climbed the three-octave peak then eased back down. Though barely awake I noticed a lovely depth of tone as I moved from scales to arpeggios. My tempo increased gradually as I waited for the smell of coffee to tell me it was time to break. Usually the coffee aroma reaches me by the time I work up to *allegro moderato*, but at *tempo vivace* I still couldn't smell it. Finally the hiss of coffee steaming to readiness reached my ears.

I put the violin down and went to investigate. I'm not a big eater and don't get food cravings the way some of my friends do. But coffee is another matter. I long for the rich black elixir, and prepare it in ritual. Each morning I grind the dark beans, shiny with oil. Then I spoon the fine grind into my stovetop espresso pot. I play scales while the liquor presses up from lower chamber to upper, awaiting the smell of its completion. While drinking, I give it my full regard. I do not leave a cup of coffee sitting on a table or desk. Like a tea ceremony I saw once at the Japanese Garden, I hold the coffee cup with both hands. I lift it up so that I can breathe the coffee before I sip, study the fine cracks in the mug, and feel the warmth in my hands. I give it full attention and believe it does the same for me, like praying and knowing that somehow God listens. After coffee, there is music.

But this morning no coffee scent tickled my nose into wakefulness. Come to think of it, I hadn't smelled the beans when I ground them either. Could the coffee be stale? But I'd smelled it the day before and every day before that. I poured, then held my special mug up with both hands to inhale; there

••• Sunday Ink 55

was nothing. No aroma of stimulus. I tried to drink, but put the cup down to go practice.

I placed the violin under my chin. Odd, I thought. My nose was not stuffy. I didn't have a cold. But music beckoned and I ceased pondering my inability to smell coffee.

The Mendelssohn had a warmth I'd never fully appreciated. My ears were fine-tuned this morning, helping my hands to form sound through the instrument. My intonation was exact, vibrato rich, bowing full, a perfect blend of skills I have worked hard to achieve. But they didn't always come so completely together. My hearing had moved up a notch in acuity, directing my hands to shape a sound that was ever so satisfying. At lunch I made a tuna sandwich and noticed I could not smell the canned fish, red onion, or kosher pickles.

Taste disappeared next, since smell had already diminished it. I knew when Julianna offered me chocolate that afternoon at our final rehearsal. Julianna played cello on the Beethoven trio. During our rehearsal break she rushed out to buy chocolate. "Beethoven drives me to it," she said, but I've noticed over the years that every piece of music Julianna played required a chocolate hit. So Leon, the pianist, and I waited and talked about electronic music and why it will never capture the sound of even one string vibrating in a room. Leon reached under the lid of the grand to pluck a low string, making his point. My ears expanded to take in the tone and rumble beneath. I heard my violin strings vibrate in resonance.

Julianna came back in and offered us each a chocolate, her eyes dilated with pleasure from the three she'd already eaten. I hesitated. "It's food of the gods," she said. "The Beethoven will be richer. Eat it." I put the chocolate in my mouth and waited. She only bought the best chocolates, the ones made by the chocolatier whose ancestors had made chocolates for the

czar of Russia. Julianna's craving never drove her to eat
Mars bars. She maintained her standards, in music and in
chocolate. I didn't tell her I tasted nothing. Only the memory
of chocolate. We played. My ears followed the trio of instru-
ments as though I were playing each one. The Beethoven sang.

I considered calling my doctor to discuss my loss of smell and
taste. But the recital stood before me and there was no time for
a doctor's appointment. My playing was breaking through to a
new level and I didn't dare stop.

The next morning, I became aware of lack of sensation in my
left hand. Carefully I pushed the strings against the neck of
the instrument and picked up the bow to play. My ears told me
I'd hit the right pitches. So I relied on hearing to tell me if I
needed more pressure on the strings or to bring the bow down
with more weight.

I continued playing, believing that feeling would return to
my hands when they warmed up. It was odd. My fingers did
everything I needed them to do. In fact, relying solely on
my hearing made my fingers more responsive than usual.
I imagined touch more thoroughly and precisely than I had
ever felt it. My control was acute. But after two hours of practice
I still had no true feeling in my fingers.

I put the violin down and examined my hands. I could see
the familiar grooves on the pads of the fingers where I'd been
holding the strings against the fingerboard. My right hand
had the usual marks creased into my thumb and fingers from
holding the bow. I sat down and stroked my hands across the
ledge of the music stand, passing my palms, then the flesh
between finger joints over the metal; I spread the pads of my
fingers out as if reading Braille embossed in the stand's
surface. The delicate whispery sound of skin against metal
described to me the cool stuccoed texture. So much so that
I imagined I felt it.

My heart beat loudly, *tempo agitato*. I rushed to the phone, found my doctor's number and punched it in. I heard the sound of each number entering the phone. *Numbness?* she inquired. *No tingling? Possibly a neurological problem, perhaps a pinched nerve, brought on by overpractice. It doesn't affect your playing? Good,* she said. *Remember to take breaks. You musicians are hard on your bodies. I'll see you next week and book you with our neurologist. You can see us both the same day. Call me if the symptoms worsen.*

My *agitato* slowed to a *moderato*. I had told my doctor and she had not panicked. I picked up the violin again. My playing was in fact better than ever. They say violinists should rely on their ears and I have, though never so entirely.

I practiced standing, as I would perform. My ears demanded a balanced sound. So I moved until the violin found the sonar center of the room. The tone swirled around me in perfect circles. My ears tracked the arc and curve of each cycle and vibration, allowing the music to build until it overpowered my practice room. Sound expanded against the acoustical tiles on the walls and ceiling.

My ears tingled. I practiced in a rapture through late afternoon and into early evening. When I emerged from the practice room, I walked to the picture window to catch the sunset improvising its wild and final solo cadenza, clouds suspended for an ephemeral moment until the contented return to tonic.

—◌෴◌—

The recital came at just the right time. My ears buzzed from shaping sound so fully and precisely. Indeed, the recital was my best. I'm not one of those performers who always claims my last recital was my best and the next one will be better. This recital was truly my best. The Mendelssohn soared, the Beethoven

trio was rich and full of passion, and the Bach unaccompanied suites were straight from the angels. My ears told me everything I needed to do, how much vibrato to create, how much bow to pull across the strings. I closed my eyes and it was just me, the violin, the music, and my ears, all working as one. This was it, I thought, the piercing ecstasy Bernini carved into the marble face of Santa Teresa of Avila. I had thought it unattainable on this earth. But now the ecstasy moved through me, swirled around me and lifted me up, even if only for a glorious instant in time.

The reviews were raves, which in the music world doesn't happen often. "Ms. Kechley achieved that rare perfection of sound that all violinists strive for. The recital was a jewel." I had to hold the newspaper just the right distance to read it.

After the recital, I stayed in for the weekend and basked in the rapture of music. I shouldered my violin in each room, allowing my ears to direct sound and adapt my playing to acoustical change. I felt like I could stay forever in this aural world, breathing the clear air of magnificent vibration.

I knew I had no excuse now for not keeping my appointment with the doctor. I went by bus. My distance vision had become too blurry for driving. I squinted out the bus window and when I spotted the ten-story clinic, I rang the bus bell, noting its remarkably sonorous chime.

My doctor examined me, asked me questions, wrote responses on her chart. "Definitely a neurological disorder. It's a good thing I got you that appointment with Dr. Morgan. This is out of my league. But don't worry, he's tops in his field."

For the next two hours, Dr. Morgan and I were together in an exam room. He asked me about the losses, when I noticed each. He asked about my profession and whether the losses affected

my performance. Then he directed me to sit on the exam table. I closed my eyes while he tapped on my wrist, my knee, my shoulder. Though I heard his every movement, and could sense his touch, I could not say that I felt it physically.

Then he rolled in a metal tray with holders for glass vials that reminded me of allergy skin tests. These contained aromatic essences of gardenia, anise, tea rose, and chili peppers. He asked me to close my eyes. I heard the thick slide of oily liquid against the glass as he waved each under my nose. I shook my head. I smelled nothing.

Next he brought in wafers for me to taste. Each came separately wrapped so its flavor would remain singular and unmixed. The number on each wrapper corresponded to numbers on his clipboard chart. I chewed slowly, waiting for my tongue to wake up and identify the familiar taste of lemon, onion, black pepper, or banana. I shook my head again and again.

"I'll need to test your vision now." He led me into a small room where I looked through a machine and read down the lines of diminishing letters. My confidence wavered after the third line. As I already knew, my distance vision had blurred but close range was fine, even sharpened slightly as the tests confirmed.

The hearing tests were last. I sat in a booth and put on earphones. He told me to push the button whenever I heard a sound, no matter how faint. I did and even through the earphones and the soundproof booth, I heard his pulse jump at what I could perceive.

We went to his office. Dr. Morgan pulled thick books and journals from his shelves and spread them across his desk. I waited as he read, listened to him turn pages, wrinkle his brow, write notes in the margin with his mechanical pencil.

Finally he spoke. "It's a rare disorder, but the symptoms are classic, for a musician, that is."

"What is the disorder?"

"Idiopathic Monoesthesia."

I listened to him pronounce the name, not sure I wanted a name to attach to my experience. "I've seen only one other case myself," he said. "A sculptor." He opened a medical file and scanned it. "Yes," he said. He pushed his glasses up and I heard the moist slide of plastic on skin. "This is how it works. The brain and nervous system weaken the senses not needed for the artist's work, and at the same time, enhance the most necessary sense to extraordinary levels. In your case it is hearing. In this clinic, no one has ever achieved your perception of pitch, volume, vibrato, timbre. You have superhuman hearing perception. Your sense of touch is processed through your hearing and I believe you will not lose any more sight because you need close vision to read music."

"I won't lose more?" I asked.

"Not likely. According to the reported cases, the losses and enhancements take place within the first week or two and then stabilize. In essence, the disorder leaves you with exactly what you need to pursue your art. And only that." He creaked back in his chair and studied me.

"Oh." I heard myself suck in air, then blow it out. "Will I hear everything in the world with such clarity?"

"No, no," he said. "It's selective. Only what you focus on. Otherwise you'd already be going crazy."

I nodded.

"The nature of IME is its selectivity. There haven't been many cases but they have all followed the same pattern. Here's an example." He picked up a journal. "A painter: the patient measured extraordinary visual acuity, able to hold both distant and close images in focus at the same time. In tests, the patient reproduced, with no optical aid, the cellular structure of an object. The patient measured complete loss of smell and taste, as well as hearing impairment." He put the journal down and looked up at me. When he folded his hands, I heard the sound of his fingers rubbing against each other, whorl on whorl. "Do you see how it works?"

"I think so," I said. "Your sculptor must have had an amazing sense of touch."

"Exactly," he said. "He did, for a time. In fact, that brings us to the subject of treatment."

"Treatment?"

"There is a drug we can administer that will effectively bring back your lost senses, but it will also bring your hearing back to what it was before. However, you need to know that the treatment is only effective within the first few weeks of initial loss, which in your case began over two weeks ago."

"I see," I said, though I probably should have said that I heard. In fact, I heard the messages just under his voice as well as the ones in it. His words said the decision was mine to make but the tonality disclosed his preference to bring back the other senses, letting the hearing drop to normal. I knew he was not a musician.

"It's a difficult choice," he said, "an intriguing predicament." His voice told me he would want to study me no matter which way I went. I heard medical journals and conference presenta-

tions in the vibrations beneath his words. "You need to decide soon." His eagerness to know bounded around me like a puppy after a ball.

I went back home. I sat on the sofa and lifted the afghan my grandmother had knitted to my cheek. I rubbed it against my skin but couldn't quite feel it. I reached for the basket on my coffee table and ran my hand across the objects it held, the sand dollar I'd found at Cape Lookout, the red scallop shell, the tiny starfish. Holding them at the right distance, I could see each clearly but the feel eluded me.

I put the basket on the table and sat still. Then on a whim, I lifted the sand dollar up to my ear. The whole room burst with sound, from thunderous waves to the sound of sand moving in the water and the infinitesimal creak of the sand dollar growing, etching a star on its underside. I held the basket to my ear and heard the cedar and raffia twine together giving off nesting sounds. The afghan brought the click of knitting needles to my ears and the soft whisper of yarn embracing yarn.

I ran into the kitchen and twisted open a jar of oregano and held it to my nose. Nothing. But against my ear, I perceived the sound of leaves slowly drying in intense sunlight, crackling slightly as they became savory and brittle. Grabbing an orange and ripping off its peel, I pushed a segment of the fruit into my mouth and ate, tasting nothing. I tore another segment in half and held it to my ear. A popping sound of individual citrus jewels burst free, released from the skin that had contained them. I could hear the juice moving slowly onto my fingers.

I washed my hands and walked into the practice room. My violin lay waiting. As I snugged it between my left shoulder and ear, I could hear the instrument's complex history of sound. The mellowed wood and taut strings carried the soft resonance of all the music ever played on it. I listened to the rich layering,

then took a breath and began to play. A rare purity of tone vibrated through the room, and for each note I heard all of the harmonics singing above the pitch and the fundamentals pulsing below it. My vibrato and bowing altered that overlay and on each note, my ears led me to reveal the perfect harmonic balance.

As I played the Bach unaccompanied suites, I heard the music, the instrument, even the composer's intent. It resounded inside me, settling right in my heart. When I finished playing I heard the gentle slide of tears on my cheeks and I knew that I could never give up this exquisite beauty.

I decided not to return to the clinic and wrote Dr. Morgan. I also enclosed two tickets to my next recital.

From then on, I listened and played the violin. I put it down only when I had to. Friends invited me to dinner and sometimes I went. They asked if I liked their lasagna and Chianti. "It's luscious," I said, but I never told them how I knew this.

I was reluctant at first to have a lover I could not feel, smell, or taste. An oboist from my chamber group kept asking me out. After making excuses through weeks of rehearsal, I finally decided to go. Perhaps it was the sweet and plaintive sound he poured into the music that seduced me. We ended up in my bed, which was good because I am used to the rumpled sounds of my own bedding and could therefore take in what he brought to my world. I listened to his skin caressing mine, his fingers on my nipples. I listened to our tongues dancing together, listened to him enter me. Our bodies made low pleasure sounds. I heard his orgasm and then mine, an explosive sound that filled my ears, the splash of landing in the middle of a lake on a hot afternoon. Afterward our affection rustled, like birds feathering into a nest.

No one except my doctor knew of my disorder. People knew I had
become nearsighted and no longer drove. They knew my playing
went to ever higher levels as I came to further understand
my gift. Sometimes they caught me listening. They say I get a
faraway look when I listen like that. But I am not far away. I am
present. I close my eyes and everything comes to me. I hear.

Susan Knox

rumpelstiltskin & associates

Dear Queen,

It's been years, but I still remember those three golden nights
we spent together. You were magnificent with your flaxen hair,
topaz eyes, and glowing skin. You were so angry at your father
for bragging to the king that you could spin straw into gold but
your fury only heightened your splendor. I was so taken with
your beauty and spirit that I spun three rooms full of straw
into gold so the king would not kill you. You promised me
your firstborn.

How have you managed all these years married to that greedy
man? I'm surprised he married you after only three rooms of
gold, but maybe he's smarter than I thought. Rumor has it you
are his financial maven and have increased the royal coffers
many times over with your shrewd stock picks, real-estate
development and venture-capital deals. Puts my ability to spin
straw into gold to shame and it's so much easier to explain.

Did you know your king had me committed? I spent seven years
in the sanitarium. The king's psychiatrists gave me a diagnosis
of multiple personality disorder because I split in two when
you guessed my name. They were totally wrong, of course, but I
bided my time. I'm not like other men, as you well know.

I must admit the weekly anger-management sessions were
fascinating. I'm not averse to learning new ways. Transmog-
rification has always been a favorite of mine. Group therapy
was a kick although the facilitator Claudia was irritating and so
insecure. Her sessions were getting boring so I decided to shake
things up a bit. I cleared Peggy's acne, reduced Ben's potbelly,

and cured Herbert's paranoia. Claudia was thrilled with the transformations but later took medical leave when she developed severe skin eruptions, mysterious bloating, and accused the director of undermining her therapy sessions.

You're probably wondering how I got released. Let's just say that once I threw away their drugs, the old magic returned.

I moved to the town that was calling me. Hollywood. A golden city with perpetual sunlight, unlimited money, and beautiful people. The perfect place for a man with my brilliance. I seek out young actors, sign them to an ironclad contract, connive to get them noticed by the right people, and control their careers as they become celebrated stars. I'm spinning their lives into gold.

I hear our son is quite talented. I guess he got the best of each of us. Now would be an excellent time to make good on that promise of yours. Do you think he could use an agent?

Regards,
R

Gregory Rumpelstiltskin
Rumpelstiltskin & Associates

Susan Knox

mirror, mirror

When did I quit looking in my mirror? It was when Snow White
was revived by the Prince's kiss and my mirror told me I was
no longer the fairest in the land. I never told my husband. I
never told him Snow White lived. Somehow he found out, but
Snow refused to come back to the castle. I wasn't invited to the
wedding and when my husband returned from the festivities he
banished me from his kingdom.

I traveled west, across the Reflection Mountains and settled in
a village in Amethyst Valley. I bought land and started growing
herbs. I know herbs. I have a magic touch with them. I grew
fields of hyssop and horehound, rosemary and rue, angelica
and belladonna. Bundles of herbs hung from my workroom
ceiling. The air shimmered with their fragrances.

I created elixirs, tinctures, and balms. My extracts cured
psoriasis, eczema, herpes, and corns. I could ease aching
limbs and creaky joints. Migraine headaches became extinct in
Amethyst Valley. I tended to my beauty. I concocted creams and
lotions infused with herbs to smooth the skin, soften wrinkles,
tighten the jaw line. The village women clamored for my
potions and I began selling my wares. I could have given them
away, but there's so much pleasure in making money.

Soon I was getting requests to mail my products far and wide.
The business flourished, almost out of hand, until I hired two
sisters who had a genius for organization and management.
Lovely girls, Ruby and Pearl, identical twins, with skin as white
as snow, hair as dark as ebony, and lips as red as blood. They
soon had my business humming. The villagers were proud to
be a part of my enterprise and vied for jobs in the business.
Ruby and Pearl created a website, infomercials, and placed my
products in department stores.

One day Ruby asked if her parents could visit. She said her father was anxious to meet me. I was flattered. From what I'd gathered from the girls' conversation, the father was important royalty in a distant kingdom.

I was in my workroom when they arrived. The father entered first. A big man with white hair and sapphire eyes, he shook my hand, and stood aside to present his wife. She took one look at me, gasped, and collapsed. We didn't know what to do at first. Pearl started artificial respiration. Ruby called for an ambulance. The king knelt by her side, chafing her wrists, calling, "Snow, Snow." I had a remedy, but it was not without side effects. I grabbed the bottle and looked to the king for permission. He nodded. I sprinkled ten drops under her tongue and waited. She began to stir. As she breathed and coughed, her skin began to wrinkle and roughen. Her daughters helped her to a chair and stared at me, their beautiful mother now an old crone.

"It couldn't be helped," I told them. "She was dying. I'll give her my most potent skin creams and rejuvenating tonics, but I can't promise full restoration."

Later that evening, I went to my leather trunk—the one I'd transported across the mountains when I left the Beryl Kingdom. I dug through silk gowns and jeweled headdresses. The mirror was near the bottom. I propped it against my bureau and I peered into the glass.

Mirror, mirror . . .

Susan Knox

stalking jack

Jack was fast asleep when the pounding started. His mother knew the teenager was a strong sleeper so she ran to his bedroom to shake him awake.

"What? Who is it?"

"Five men in dark grey uniforms and black leather boots. They parked a black panel truck across the end of the driveway," his mother said.

Jack pulled on some sweats and ran downstairs. He peered through the door's window. Five gold badges glinted in the sun.

"Homeland Security," one of them yelled. "Open up." Jack opened the door. The men rushed into the entry hall as though they were responding to a five-alarm fire.

"Where's the garden?"

"Out back, through the kitchen. Wait a minute! Don't you need a search warrant?"

"Homeland Security doesn't have time for search warrants. Homeland Security is responsible for protecting America and her citizens. Homeland Security is all that stands between peace and violence in the homeland." The men hurried to the kitchen.

"What do you want with our garden?" asked Jack, close on their heels.

"We had a report of a large, dark, bearded man, probably Middle Eastern, in your garden. You know what that means."

"I'm not sure I do."

"Terrorist!"

Jack laughed. "Well he was a terror all right, but I don't think I'd call him a terrorist."

"You knew him?" The five men pivoted to stare at Jack.

These guys were scary. "I knew of him," Jack backpedaled. "He had a reputation."

"We hear he had an unusual device. A fast-growing plant. Could be used to ruin our national food supply by overrunning slower-growing crops."

Jack could have explained he traded his mother's milking cow for the beans. He could have reassured them there were only five beans and he had planted them all. He could have revealed the giant died when he lost his footing on the beanstalk. He could have confessed he rolled the body into the fast-moving Riffle River. He could have informed them he cut down the beanstalk, pulverized it, and carted the mulch to the community dump. But Jack was more afraid of these government agents than he had ever been of the giant.

"Go ahead and look around. There's not much to see but Mom's roses."

The men flung open the back door and clattered down the patio steps. Jack and his mother watched from the doorway as the agents split up and began prodding the earth with slim

metal rods.

"Jack," his mother whispered, putting her hand on Jack's arm. "What if they search the barn? What if they find Odila? They'll accuse us of undermining the gold standard and trying to ruin the economy."

"We'll just pray she doesn't lay an egg while they're here."

Arleen Williams

excerpt from **moving mom,** a memoir in progress

A small table stands in the middle of the large activity room. Sunlight shines bright through the tall windows. White tablecloth. Folded washcloths. Colorful caddies of nail polish, cold cream, and hair curlers. Chairs form a wide circle around the table. As the clock inches toward 2:00 PM, these chairs fill, one by one, with residents. Some roll in seated in their own chairs, others enter with walkers, and still others, like my mother, walk with brisk, confident steps. All come with the curiosity of young children, not fully understanding the words: Spa Day. But willing, even eager, for the attention.

This is Mom's first Spa Day. My mother is a woman who has never, in her 84 years, visited a spa. Throughout her life, her many years of work and mothering, her nails were short and efficient. Her hair was cut, and at times permed, only to make it easy to handle. With nine kids, anything that simplified life was important.

Was she always this way, my mother? Was there a time in her high school or college days, as a young nurse, as a flight attendant, when she gloried in her beauty, when she pampered her skin, her hair, her nails? When she showed off her natural assets?

Who was my mother before she became my mother and slowly lost herself?

It's Mom's turn at the spa table. A headband holds back her silver hair as a young volunteer massages cold cream into her wrinkles.

"Where's my daughter?" I hear her ask as I walk through the open door.

"She's gone to your room for a minute, Sally. She'll be right back."

"I'm here, Mom," I say, a hand on her shoulder. "I was putting your coat away."

"Do you know where my room is? I can show you."

"You showed me, Mom. It's okay. I put your coat there."

"That's good," she says.

She looks up into my eyes, the cold cream glistening in the winter sunlight, her grey-blue eyes unshielded by glasses. I see trust and love and confusion.

"I need to get back to work now, Mom," I lie. An innocent lie, I tell myself. A lie that will allow me to leave while she is fully occupied, distracted by cold cream and gentle fingers.

I wonder what it would be like to massage cold cream into my mother's face, to feel her skin under my fingers without the plastic surgical gloves worn by the volunteer. Would it make a difference to her? My skin against hers? Would she even know now that my skin, my fingertips, are of her, from her?

I take my mother's hands in mine. Small, birdlike bones. I feel each of them under paper-thin, dry skin. Delicate, easily bruised skin. Transparent skin. I remember years before, when I was living in Venezuela, I was called *La Rana Platanera*—the banana frog—a tropical species with such transparent skin that the inner workings of the body are visible to the naked eye. Or so I was told. My blue veins showing through thin, white skin earned me a nickname that I now gift to my mother's hands. The hands of a *rana platanera*.

I feel her small hands in mine, and I remember the pudgy soft hands of my daughter. Now that she is an adult, my daughter and I don't hold hands anymore. Now her fingers are long and slender, no longer the pudgy, chubby fingers of a toddler. Now she has rounded, sometimes polished nails, no longer the French acrylics of her early teens.

I've never seen artificial color on my mother's nails. Trimmed short in her years of nursing and mothering, these ten nails have now grown long and hard, almost clawlike. A novelty for a woman who never had nails. Difficult to cut and file. The chore had become overwhelming for her, and yet she would not allow me to do it for her or to take her for a manicure.

Now it is different. Now it's Spa Day. Now my mother has long pink fingernails.

"This is my sister," she tells the volunteer, who continues to massage cold cream into her skin.

"Your daughter?" the volunteer responds.

"Yes," I say.

Then I lean forward and wrap my mother in my arms, fearful of hugging too tight, of bruises and broken bones. "I'll see you soon, Mom," I say. "I love you."

"I love you too," she says.

I hurry toward the exit and enter the code that allows me to leave, fearful that her comfort level is temporary, that at some point she'll decide she's tired of this game and wants to go home.

But then, maybe not. Maybe she's relieved. Free of fear, surrounded by warm, gentle care providers, no longer bearing the weight of responsibility.

Maybe her words in the garden a few hours earlier are her new truth.

⁓

This is my third visit in the two weeks since my sisters, our husbands, and I took Mom from her home. Each time we begin the visit with a tour. Each time my mother shows me her room, her bathroom, her closet, her window, her heater.

"It's hot in here," she says.

"It sure is," I agree. For as long as I can remember, Mom has complained about being cold. Now she's too warm.

"It works like this," she says, turning the dial of the small wall heater farther into the red zone.

"Maybe it should go this way, Mom. Blue is cooler. Red is hotter."

"Okay," she says.

She shows me each framed photo on the shelf and the dresser. "This is my family," she says.

"Yup," I say. "That's Doreen and Michael. And there's Dad." I rattle through the names of our large family, pointing, reminding. Trying to retie the fragile string of memory and give her back the names and relationships she struggles to grasp.

"And this one is my dad." She holds a photograph of my father.

"Ray," I say. "Your husband. My dad."

As she returns the frame to the dresser, I seek distraction. "What else do you want to show me, Mom?"

"Will you be warm enough?" she asks.

"Sure. Let's go outside."

The sun is bright as we walk the long semicircle sidewalk that surrounds three-quarters of the building. Only the front entrance lies beyond the security of the solid wood fence that encloses the facility.

"It's so beautiful," I say. "It'll be even prettier when the bushes and flowers begin to bloom this spring."

"There's lots of cars," she says. "Up there." She points to the parking lot of the adjacent building on the hillside above.

"Yes, but the fence keeps them out."

"And the gate," she adds.

"The gate keeps you safe."

"It doesn't open," she says. She shakes the gate with both hands.

"That's right. It keeps you safe," I repeat.

We reach the end of the semicircle and turn to retrace our steps in the opposite direction.

"And my house?" she asks.

I freeze. Here it is. The beginning of trouble. "It's okay," I say.

"Is there a sign?" she asks, struggling to find the words.

My thirty years of ESL teaching serve me well. I complete her thoughts, her sentences, when words escape her. "No, Mom. There's no sign."

"I mean, is it . . ."

"Sold? No, it's not sold."

"Is there anybody there?"

"No, Mom, nobody's there. But, I'd like to use it sometimes if that's okay with you."

"You can have it," she says. "I live here now."

I key my way through the front security doors and into Mom's new home in the early afternoon of an unusually warm early spring day. The stale recirculated air assaults my senses. Thick institutional air. The kind of air that makes me want to throw open the doors and windows for even the slightest whisper of a breeze. I long for the fresh air of my mother's house in Grayland.

I walk the wide halls encircling the center square of the single-story building. The doors to each of the four wings are blocked open in a feeble attempt to improve air circulation. I make my way to the large activity room expecting to find a semicircle of the aged engaged in some type of activity, a religious service or singing or maybe just watching a movie on the large flat-screen television.

But as I enter the large room, I find it empty, not a single elderly soul to be seen. I move on to the next room, a smaller gathering room with long tables for puzzles, cards, bingo, crafts. There I find a handful of women with one of the activity coordinators, but no Mom. I retrace my steps. I check the dining room and the small sitting room. Still no Mom. When I reach her room, I give a gentle rap and try to turn the knob. Locked. I didn't even know the doors locked. Later one of the caregivers assures me that they can easily be opened with any straight pin or nail. But at that particular moment, I am surprised and concerned. After a few more tries and a few louder knocks, I feel those little hairs on the back of my neck, the alert of panic. Where the hell is my mother?

And then the door opens. My mother stands before me in a long-sleeve, bright-red fleece sweater smoothing her hair with one hand and rubbing the sleep out of her eyes with the other.

"Oh, it's you," she says.

"I'm sorry, Mom," I say. "I didn't mean to wake you. I didn't know."

Know what? That my 84-year-old mother naps like a two-year-old every afternoon between lunch and dinner? I wonder how long she sleeps. I wonder if she dreams, what she dreams, where her mind goes when she is asleep. I wonder if she has the night terrors that haunted my own two-year-old so long ago.

"It's okay," she says.

"I was wondering if you'd like to go out for a drive, Mom. It's a beautiful day," I say as I walk into her stuffy bedroom.

"Okay," she says. "But I have to go to the bathroom."

"And you probably need a short-sleeve shirt. It's warm out there."

"Really?"

"Yup."

"But I'm cold."

"You won't be outside." I pull a short-sleeve shirt from her closet and hand it to her as she enters the bathroom. "Put that on, Mom. You can put a sweater over the top if you get cold."

A few minutes later, she's ready. "Let's go have an adventure," I say.

"Do you have a car?" Mom asks.

"Sure do."

"I don't have one."

"Well, it's a good thing I do, then." I dangle the keys in front of her like a dog treat in front of a hungry hound. "What do you think? Do you want to go out for a drive?"

"I don't have a car," she says.

I take her hand, and we walk out to the parking lot.

"I'm hot," she says.

"Yup," I say with a laugh. "It's a hot day in Seattle."

"Is this your Dad's car?" she asks.

"Nope, it's mine."

"Did I tell Mom where I was going?"

"Yup, they know we're going on an adventure."

I head toward the small waterfront town of Edmonds thinking that she'll enjoy the familiarity of the beach, the waves rolling up the sand and gulls overhead.

"Do they know where I am?"

"Yup, we told them we'd be back by dinnertime."

"Okay."

After several false turns, I find my way into Edmonds and pull into a parking spot facing the beach. The spring sunlight dances on the cold water of Puget Sound as a ferry docks at the terminal. We count cars as they stream off the large boat.

"Did we tell them?"

"Yes, Mom. We told them. Are you ready for a cup of tea?"

She looks confused. "Tea? But I don't have any."

"That's okay. We can get some."

"But I don't have any." She pats her pockets, looks at the floor of the car and around her seat.

"Money?" I ask.

"Yes."

"No worries. I've got money."

"But I don't have anything."

"It's my treat."

I maneuver into another perfect parking spot just across from a corner coffee shop and the beautiful little Edmonds water fountain. As we settle into a cozy corner with warm tea between us, I know the time is right. I know I need to try one last time to understand this woman who is my mother. With a deep breath, I begin.

"I'm writing another book, Mom," I tell her, knowing full well she has no memory of the first book I wrote or of the conversation we had a few years before in the Westport pizza restaurant when I told her I was writing about Maureen.

"That's nice," she says.

"It's about you."

"Me? Why me?"

"Well," I stammer. "Because you're my mom, you know, and because I like to write."

"Okay," she says. My confusion seems to satisfy her, so I forge on.

"I was wondering, Mom, what's really, really important? What should I be sure to include in this story about you?"

I know I can't ask her what she remembers. I can't use that dreaded word. Instead, I stick to *important*. "What's important to you, Mom?" I repeat. "What's been important in your life?"

I watch as her expression changes, as a distance enters her face. She is far away from me, from the little coffee shop. She relaxes into the high-backed velvet chair, her head tilted up, her eyes to the ceiling.

"Oh, I don't think about that." There is a long pause before she continues. "I don't know," she says. "It's been a good life."

We sit in silence for a long while enjoying those few words, the warmth of our tea and the spring sunshine, the faint sounds of water flowing in the fountain beyond the window, and the rich heady fragrance of fresh ground coffee. She stares into the world above her as I wait in silence, unsure if she will say anything more and unwilling to interrupt her thoughts.

"Did we tell Mom where we were going?" she asks.

"Yes, we told them we'd be back by dinner." And I know, in that moment, that we will never again speak of this story I am writing.

"Where's the car?" she asks as I help her from her chair.

"Right there, at the curb."

"The red one?"

I look up and down the street. There's no red car anywhere to be seen. "Nope," I say. "The green one. Or is it blue? What do you think, Mom? I never know what to call it."

"Blue," she says. "Blue's my best color."

"So, now we have to figure out how to get back," I say as I hold the car door and she sinks into the seat, clinging to the window for support.

I drive out of Edmonds and head north on Highway 99, but somehow I forget the cross street. Is it 188th or 148th or 128th? Numbers. I think of myself as numerically challenged, but as I struggle to remember names as well, I fear that I am becoming my mother. I push the thought from my head and arbitrarily take a right turn on 148th. After numerous false turns on endless residential streets that seem to curl back onto themselves, I pull to a stop and look at my mother.

"I have no idea where we are. I think we're lost."

"Lost," she echoes.

"Yeah, but it's all part of the adventure, right? I know if I keep heading this way, we'll hit Interstate 5, then I'll be able to figure it out."

"Okay," she says. "You're a good driver."

"I had good teachers."

"Who?"

"You and Dad taught me, remember? In the riding ring."

I realize my mistake before the word is out of my mouth. Like a slap in the face, I used the word *remember*. I tested her memory. She clams up, desperately trying to *remember*. I keep talking, determined to explain away her confusion.

"I drove around and around and around in circles in the horse-riding ring at the first Issaquah house. Sometimes I drove with you and sometimes with Dad until I was good enough to go on the road. Crap. Should we go left or right? What'd you think?"

"That way," she says, her finger pointing to the left. "Did Dad teach me to drive too?"

"Maybe," I say. My heart is heavy with the knowledge that my dad, her husband, her dad, my grandfather, have all become one in her muddled memory.

"Now we're really lost," I say.

"Oh, good," she laughs.

"I hope you don't miss dinner."

"I'm not hungry," she says. "You make me laugh."

"Good. Now if I can just find a way out of here."

Just then, I see the interstate crossing over the road ahead of us. "Hoorah! Now I sort of know where I am," I say, and Mom claps her appreciation. "North or south? Are we too far north or too far south? I guess we'll head north."

"Okay," she says.

"Wrong again," I say a few minutes later when the large green EVERETT sign looms overhead. "How'd we get this far north? I could've sworn we were too far south."

"I don't know," she says. "You're driving."

I steal a glance in her direction as I stop at the foot of the off-ramp and prepare to make a U-turn. She is smiling, a huge mischievous grin painted across her wrinkles. A few minutes later I take the correct exit and, in moments, pull to a stop in front of her building.

"Home, sweet home," I say.

Susan Knox

i didn't know

"I woke up this morning and I didn't know where I was," my mother says. "It scared me." We're sitting on the sofa in her new living quarters at Copeland Oaks Retirement Center in Sebring, a small town in northeastern Ohio. Mom recently transferred from her apartment to assisted-living because she couldn't remember to take her medications for asthma, acid reflux, epilepsy, edema, and rheumatism. Senile dementia has grasped my mother by the hand, but there aren't any pills for dementia; there's no way to stop her slip from reality.

I slide closer to her as she turns her body to face me. She is 85. Her body is thick now, her ankles swollen, her fingers bent with arthritis. Her round brown eyes survey my face and I see unspoken questions in hers. I murmur comforting sounds, humming noises, because I don't know what to say to her and because that's the way we handle emotional issues in our family—we don't talk about them.

Years ago I used to tease Mom when she worried about getting Alzheimer's. I told her it wouldn't matter if she got it because she wouldn't know. But she does know. I didn't know that she would know. She knows.

Her new rooms, a bedroom and living room, are lovely—large and sunny with picture windows that frame green Ohio hills. It's springtime, an especially pretty spring in 2001 with pale pink blossoms on the cherry trees outside her window, their scent drifting under her barely opened window. We exchange news about the family. I offer a sketch of my life in downtown Seattle and Mom tells me the laundry service is her favorite perk in assisted-living. We leaf through the Maryland Square shoe catalog and order her a pair of tan shoes with Velcro

fasteners because she has trouble tying her shoes. I pull out a synopsis of a book I'm writing on financial basics for college students. She reads it and says, "This is good, Susan. You should go on television to talk about these issues."

I take in her praise and appreciation and smile, pleased.

"Grandma wants me to come to the farm," she says. "Help her put up peach preserves."

Dementia is a tangle of memories. Sometimes the brain smoothes them out; sometimes the tangles tighten. I decide to try to straighten this memory.

"Mom," I say gently, "Your grandmother is dead. Remember?"

"Oh yes," she giggles. "How silly of me."

So dear. So sweet. So sad.

I am following her, ignorant about her disease, her aging process, her deterioration, not knowing what will come and if I will be able to help her. This is new territory for both of us and she can't guide me. It makes me wonder what will come with my old age.

Mom loves good food and long car rides. I want to give her a treat, something to break up her routine. We'll go to the Hearth and Eagle in Hanoverton and eat lobster with drawn butter. We'll drive down Main Street in Minerva, past the beauty shop she used to own, stop by the family farm, drop in at Dutch and Betty's, her friends of fifty years. Maybe this will perk her up, engage her mind, stymie the dementia. I stop by the nurse's desk to pick up her pills.

"Let's see," I say looking in my purse, "where can I put these so

I don't forget to give them to her?"

"Got a bit of Mom's problem?" A nurse's aide speaks to me in a sarcastic tone. I look up at her. Is this how she talks to my mother? Should I call her on this or will she later take it out on my mother? How does the staff treat my mother when I'm not around? Do they respect her? Do they appreciate her creativity and sense of humor? Do they realize she likes someone to rub her feet in the evening before she goes to bed? I suddenly recognize she is at the mercy of strangers—vulnerable and powerless.

A few months after my visit, my brother Tom calls. Tom lives in Cleveland, seventy miles from the retirement home and has taken over as Mom's proxy.

"The head nurse at Copeland called. She said Mom is slipping more and more into another world," Tom says. "I visited her yesterday. Mom said she went to a farm for three weeks to help with the harvest. She said she cooked for the hired hands. Then she told me one of these days she would walk to my house for a visit."

This frightens us. We picture her wandering back-country roads in her nightgown.

I fly to Ohio to visit her and arrive after dinner. We watch television for an hour, but she doesn't want to talk. I say goodnight and remind Mom I will come by in the morning so we can go to breakfast together. This has been our pattern since she moved to Copeland Oaks six years ago.

The next morning I arrive at the nurse's station on my mother's floor.

"Hi. I'm here to take my mother to breakfast."

The nurse looks up. "She's already eaten. We take them to the cafeteria at seven."

Mom used to get up at nine when she lived in her apartment. I walk down the hall to my mother's rooms wondering why the staff gets them up so early.

"Good morning," Mom says. "Ready for breakfast?"

I decide to say nothing. As we wait for the elevator Mom suddenly whirls around and looks up at me like a frightened child on the first day of school.

"I don't remember how to go to the cafeteria."

"It's okay," I say. "I remember the way."

She smiles at me and looks relieved. When we get to the cafeteria, she orders toast for breakfast remarking that she's not very hungry this morning.

I want to take Mom for a drive. I've rented a Cadillac for its high-wide seats so Mom can more easily get into the car. I hold her hands to steady her as she lowers her body, slowly, carefully, into the leather seat. I lift her legs and help her swivel to face forward. I drive the country roads. She is silent. She stares straight ahead, not looking at the scenery or pointing out crop plantings, flower gardens, weather conditions—details she used to notice. She doesn't want to go to the movies, one of the fun things we do together. The last movie we saw together was *Clueless* and, as she would say, we both got a kick out of it. She has trouble walking and her legs seem weak. We can't go to her favorite restaurant because there are stairs to the dining room and she can't lift her legs to get up the steps. She is so quiet.

I ache for my mother. I ache for the long telephone conversations

we no longer have. I ache for the laughter we used to share. I ache for her kiss on my cheek and a quick hug.

After I take her back to her room, I walk to the main nursing office to see Bridgett, the head nurse.

Bridgett is stationed behind her desk, her hands flat on the desktop. "Your mother's situation is deteriorating. She is restless at night. We've found her roaming the hallways looking for her husband."

Dad died twenty years ago.

Bridgett leans forward. "We are not equipped for this behavior in assisted-living. We can't guarantee her safety. She might wander off the grounds, get lost. You'll have to move her to the nursing wing, soon."

Bridgett reminds me of a staff sergeant in the Army who strictly follows the rules.

Tom and I search for alternatives. Mom is happy in her rooms. We believe the move will be a wrench for her. Can she be monitored in some way so the staff will know if she leaves the assisted-living area? Is there some kind of positioning device that could track her location? Bridgett says no.

Can we hire around-the-clock care? Bridgett says it's never been done before. In Bridgett's book, that means no. I contact my Aunt Mildred's friend, Winifred Clausing, at the Fort Belvoir Retirement Home in Virginia. Winifred arranged for private care when Mildred was moved to the nursing facility.

"I hired staff through Mildred's nursing home," Winifred tells me. "They took responsibility for scheduling nurses' aides and paying the wages. It's almost impossible to do on your own."

Tom travels on business and I live far away. We can't hire people, monitor them, ensure they show up, pay their wages, handle payroll taxes; we need an organization to do this for us. We look for a temp agency to provide health-care personnel for Mom's daily care. We find nothing.

"Maybe I should bring her out to Seattle," I tell Tom. "Maybe I can locate a facility that can better deal with her condition."

Tom reminds me I tried to get her to move to Seattle six years ago, but she wanted to stay in Ohio. He's worried about how a change away from familiar people and surroundings will affect her. She has lived within a twenty-mile radius of Sebring all her 85 years. She has many friends who regularly visit; she enjoys the seasons; she predicts the weather by looking at the sky. A change in venue may alarm her, worsen the dementia. We decide not to move her across the country.

There is no good alternative.

Tom drives to Sebring.
Tom and Mom sit in her living room.
Tom tells her.
"Must I?" She asks.
Tom nods yes.
She bows her head.

She moves to Crandall, the nursing wing. She brings a few things with her: framed family photos, her favorite Hummel figurine—a smiling girl in a blue dress with a kerchief on her head—and a hand-knitted throw. She leaves behind her oil paintings, her new blue-flowered sofa, her grandmother's cherry platform rocker, her pillow-top mattress, her goose down pillows, her hand-painted Victorian lamp.

She no longer has a sunny room. The view of rolling hills and

Japanese cherry trees is gone. Her one small window overlooks
a parking lot. Her narrow room holds a hospital bed, reclining
chair, and chest of drawers.

Her food is chosen for her, portion-controlled. It is served
in the dining room on a stainless-steel plate with three
indentations for the food. She sits at a small table with three
other patients. They focus on eating. No one talks.

She wears a bracelet that sets off alarms if she wanders out
the front door.

She stops walking. She relies on a wheelchair.

Chocolate holds no desire. Candy goes untouched.
She puts away her hearing aids. She doesn't answer her
telephone.

An aide takes her to the bathroom. An aide bathes her. An aide
dresses her.

I don't know why, a year later, at 7 PM on a Monday evening
when I walk into Crandall Nursing Home and see my mother
asleep in her wheelchair parked in the hallway, I know what she
wants from me.

I'd driven to Sebring from the Pittsburg Airport—a two-hour
trip on the Interstate cutting through farmland and rolling
green hills. It is late June. Wheat and oat fields sprout bright-
green stalks, corn is about a foot high, the air smells fresh
and sweet.

But I barely registered my surroundings. I was thinking about
my mother surviving a second bout with pneumonia in the last
six weeks. When the nursing home called my brother Tom for

instructions, he said, yes, of course, take her to the hospital.
I concurred. It didn't occur to either of us that there was an
alternative. When one has pneumonia, one goes to the hospital
for antibiotics, intravenous fluids, oxygen. I had yet to hear the
aphorism "pneumonia is an old person's friend."

The nursing home's thermostat is set at eighty degrees. I wipe
my forehead with a tissue. I feel as though I am in a sauna.
The overhead fluorescent lights are so bright I want to shade
my eyes with my hand.

I kneel on the brown tweed carpet beside my sleeping mother.
I see the white, brown, black flecks in the carpet. Its ugliness
makes me sad. Mom's chin rests on her chest in the manner
of a person who has bowed to the inevitable. She is breathing
shallowly and her skin is pale.

"Mom," I say, grasping her still elegant hand with its perfectly
proportioned slim fingers and slender palm. Her diamond
wedding ring glitters on her ring finger. A brown old-age
spot—round and raised on the back of her left hand near her
thumb—mirrors the one on my hand as though we are twins
sharing the same physical characteristics.

She looks up. "Susan," she says greeting me with love in
her voice.

I do not expect this. I don't expect her to recognize me. Tom
had warned me her mental faculties had declined. It is as
though she cut through the misfirings and clutter in her brain
to a moment of clarity. Tears come to my eyes. I tell her I came
to stay for a few days, to make sure she was okay. I chatter on a
bit, become silent as she falls back to sleep.

Then Mom raises her head in the manner of a great animal
making one last effort and says in a strong voice, "Oh, Susan,"
and is quiet again.

I know what she is telling me. I know what she needs from me. She is telling me she is tired: tired of ambulance trips, tired of hospital beds, tired of nurses looking for a vein. She is tired of being bound to a bed and a wheelchair.

A nurse's aide walks over to us and tells me it is time to get Mom into bed. She asks me to wait outside her room while she changes her diaper. I lean against the wall in the hallway, my blouse sticking to my back, and listen to a voice drifting from another corridor pleading, "Help me, please, help me," over and over again.

Mom is tucked in bed when I walk into her room. I sit beside her and touch her hand. Suddenly her legs begin to move vigorously back and forth as though she is walking. She thrusts her legs from under the blanket and tries to swing them over the side. I quiet her. I tell her she must rest, that she isn't strong enough to stand.

"Yes, I know. I don't know why I do that."

She wants to move on.

She falls asleep and I sit with the nurse's aide for a few minutes. Stacy tells me she visited Mom in the hospital, brought her flowers and a teddy bear. I am touched by her thoughtfulness and think she must love my mother too. We talk about the atmosphere in the hospital—cold, noisy, sterile. Then Stacy says something that changes everything. She says, "I was shocked when you sent her back to the hospital the second time."

I look at her for a moment and ask, "Doesn't everyone go to the hospital when they have pneumonia?"

Stacy shakes her head no, says many people stay at the nursing home preferring to die in familiar surroundings. "We don't

leave them alone. If family isn't here we stay with them," she
tells me.

We often have help for the major events in life. When I started
menstruating at ten, my mother had prepared me in advance
and guided me through those unsettling moments. My first
boyfriend in high school upset me when he didn't call as he
promised. My mother advised me some boys are like that
and asked if I was willing to have him treat me that way.
My mother was with me when my first child was born and
helped me become a mother. But now my mother is ill, wishing
to die and I am alone. It is up to me to enter this unknown
territory, seek out knowledge and advice. I hardly knew where
to turn when the opening came from this young nurse's aide.
Imagine thinking there is a strict protocol for dealing with
illness and death and then one day someone hands you a new
script and suddenly you know you have options—humane,
loving options. The air moves, the day seems brighter. *Thank you*
my mother silently whispers.

I seek out the head nurse. We stand at the nurses' station in the
middle of the building where hallways radiate out like spokes on
a wheel. I don't remember the nurse's name but I do remember
her kind manner, soft voice, and willingness to listen to me as
I alternately cry and tell her my concerns. She reiterates what
Stacy told me, adding that Hospice is used to ensure the patient
is comfortable and pain-free. She confirms patients do not
die alone.

I go outside, find a wooden bench shaded by a maple tree, and

call Tom. I tell him what I've learned.

"Would we feel guilty if we didn't send her back to the hospital the next time?" I ask Tom.

"I don't know. Maybe. What do you think Mom would want?"

Tom and I had previously refused a feeding tube knowing she would not want that kind of intervention.

"I believe she would stay at Crandall with the people who have been caring for her the past year and a half."

Tom and I talk for an hour examining all the issues. Finally we decide.

I return to the head nurse. I tell her I do not want my mother to die in the hospital. I tell her my brother and I have decided she should stay at Crandall if she develops pneumonia again. She nods and makes a note on Mom's chart.

It is time to return to Seattle. I kiss Mom goodbye, tears in my eyes, not able to tell her what is in my heart. She looks at me intently as I glance back while leaving her room—a look I remember from times past. A look that says don't let me down.

She died four weeks later, July 28, 2003, a month short of her 88th birthday.

I was not with her when she died. I wish I could have been by her bed, to witness her last moments, to touch her hand, to tell her it was all right to go, but it happened so quickly even Tom couldn't get to her in time. But I hold on to that last visit, my time with her, the moment she raised her head and said, "Oh, Susan," her greeting a farewell.

Pamela Hobart Carter

apology

I apologize for finding this dog to shadow
you even as you pace the attic from desk
to window, you and he, a pair now, contemplating
those tough computer programming issues
at which dogs notoriously shine.
He accompanies your every step. I'm sorry
he curls into a protective C near the head
of the stairs in case an intruder prowls
through the rest of the house to find you;
protects you in his guardian curl but fails
to bark unless, of course, the intruder thinks
to use the doorbell and then, I'm sorry I
brought home this dog who joins the clamor
of the clapper and dashes and woofs
and raises the roof. I am sorry I chose this dog
who walks with a loose leash by your side, calmer
than a summer wind, calmer than the yogi,
tail swinging, mouth in a big, wide laugh
and you must walk and walk and walk him
and he draws you outdoors in black, in wet.
I am sorry this dog lures you from your work;
this dog holds you close to home; this dog
empties your pocketbook; this dog compels
you to love him. I'm sorry.

Janet Yoder

the helmet

He picked up the helmet. It glistened in the lights from *Club Salsa,* so shiny I could read the red neon letters in its blackness. The words were backward. He smiled, placed the helmet over my head, and strapped it tight under my chin. I'd just met him, loved his dark eyes and his dancing, our dancing. That was our time together, like breathing each other's air.

He bent his head to kiss me, and I could feel his hands touch the back of the helmet. We rode off toward the lake. The streets were empty. It was the middle of the night and we roared through the quiet, the time when people are asleep and if you're awake, you've got it all to yourself, the whole world.

We raced along the lake. We leaned into the curves, my hands tight around him. Cool air. Intoxicating speed. Body-to-body close. Perfection. Then perfection skidded away, spun out. Perfection leaned against gravity. Perfection flew. And pounded into the ground. Only the engine screamed on.

....

I landed on the grass. He hit a tree. They said the helmet saved my life. I only got scratches, bruises, and a stiff neck. They checked me out of the hospital by morning. He was moved to intensive care.

....

I wait outside intensive care in a white room. I sit on a metal chair with a red plastic seat. His girlfriend is here. She says she's his girlfriend. "I've been with Eddie for years," she says, "until

recently." Her mouth curls down and she speaks like she is the
queen, "I am thankful you are all right." What she means is
*why did you take his helmet? Why aren't you in intensive care? Why were you
with him?*

She's a cool number, tall and blonde. Her skin looks so pale
I wonder if she ever goes out in the sun. Her sea-green dress
comes down almost to her feet when she's sitting. She studies
me with ice-blue eyes, my dancing clothes—heels and tight
black dress—and my Magenta Magic nail polish. She pulls
her eyes back like she's not really seeing me. Her tied-back
hair and careful way of talking make me guess she's a lawyer
or an accountant or an executive. I don't tell her I work at the
plumbing supply place, filling orders for shower nozzles, brass
spigots, and custom color tubs. I don't mention I like teasing
the plumbers and contractors that come in. I don't think she
would get that.

I try to imagine them together. I wonder if his dark heat could
melt her ice a little. She's got the deep freeze turned up high
for me.

He didn't mention having a girlfriend. He held me close, and
sometimes he swung me out. We danced cha-cha, rumba,
cumbia, mambo, and meringue, moving right through the beat
of the conga, claves, and timbales until we embodied the music.
He had some coke and we snorted a little, just to make things
sparkle, like the white of his teeth and the spotlight bouncing
off the rim of the bongo.

I only went there to dance, not to meet someone. Dancing
is how I know I'm really here, my way of pinching myself to
make sure I'm awake. I need a partner who knows the rhythms
and the steps. Moving to this music is a way of talking without
opening your mouth. I was raised with these dances. My parents
didn't want me to learn Spanish. They never spoke it around

me. But I learned their dances at parties for every birthday, First Communion, graduation, and wedding. Dance was my first language. I moved away from my family and I'm not sorry for that, but I miss salsa. Sometimes I go out to feel fluent, to do something I do really well, something I can perform with a partner, different partners. It doesn't matter.

This time, it did matter. Eddie and I were doing more than just speaking the same language. We were saying things to each other. Meeting him was like finding a surprise gift from a long-lost aunt, the best gift I've ever gotten.

When the club closed, we got on the bike. I didn't ask to. He said *let's ride down to the lake and feel the night air.* I wrapped my arms around him, felt the soft leather of his jacket. We roared and followed the curves, leaning one way then the other, as if we were still dancing, still moving in a conga line. The lights shimmered across the water, winking at us, inviting us to go even faster.

....

Now I'm in this white room, and the girlfriend is across from me. They let her go see him. Maybe she's whispering to him about how she forgives him, how they belong together, how they can start over.

She comes back out and sits down again. "You don't have to stay," she says in the same way my first-grade teacher used to announce, "It's time for everyone to go home." She doesn't go, though. She's still dressed in the sea-green number looking like she spent last night in the waiting room.

I wonder how they were in bed. It doesn't look like their bodies could even speak the same language. Hers would speak some stiff language that sounds like mouthfuls of oatmeal. His body would speak a rolling language, where rhythm poured out of every part of him, even his fingernails and eyebrows. They would have needed one of those translators like they have at the United Nations, someone who could speak both languages and go back and forth between them. Maybe that's why opposites attract, because they like the translation, because they like space between what they say, the space between their bodies.

He and I didn't need that space. We spoke right to each other with nothing between us. We didn't make love. I knew we'd be good together because of the way we danced the tango. He locked his hips into mine and moved with that slow tension. No space. No translation. Heat.

....

At home the helmet sits on my dresser. I see its shiny blackness from my bed. At night, it takes on a glow. From inside the face hole, his dark eyes watch me. I get up to turn the helmet around and my fingers follow the scrapes and dents in the curved surface. I rub my hands over it like reading Braille. I crawl back in bed. Under the covers, I cannot fall asleep.

....

After work, I return to the hospital. I carry the helmet because it's not mine and I couldn't just keep it, not without offering it back. I see the ceiling lights of the hospital reflect bright white off its blackness.

"I don't want to see that thing," the girlfriend says, looking away from the helmet like it's something dirty, something that will hurt her. I slide it under my chair and stare at her. She looks like she slept in the waiting room again and her tiredness hangs under her eyes. "Why are you coming here anyway?" she asks. "You can't see him."

"Why not?"

"Look, I know he picked you up. We've been having a hard time. But we go way back. I've known Eddie sixteen years. You just met him that night. There's no reason for you to be here."

"I owe him," I said. "He gave me his helmet."

"Well, you shouldn't have taken it."

"He put it on me."

"God, I wish he'd never bought that motorcycle."

"He rode it like a king."

"He's lying in a coma because of it. That and his midlife crisis. You're just a small part of it. You don't know him."

"Maybe you don't know everything about him either." I cross my legs. She looks down at my ankle bracelet like it's made out of spiders crawling around my leg.

"Believe me. I know Eddie." She says those last three words real slow and her eyes stare into mine.

I shrug, slide the helmet out from under my chair and head for the elevator.

....

I take the helmet home and place it on my dresser again. After dark, his eyes look out at me. They never close. He's asking me something.

....

It's early, before work, and I return to the hospital. She's there, standing guard. I can tell she's been home this time. Her hair is wet from the shower and she's changed into pale blue.

"Hi," I say. She nods at me, like she expected me to show up.

"Are you going to come every day?" She crosses her arms, as if closing a door in my face. "It doesn't do any good. He's in a coma."

"I'd like to see him."

"He's in intensive care. They can't have just anybody wandering around back there."

"I'm not just anybody. I was with him, and I want to see him." I remember his eyes looking out from the helmet and it makes my voice strong, even as I stand before the ice queen. "Why don't you arrange it?"

She looks at me a long time. She walks over to the entrance to intensive care. She hesitates at the door with her hands in her pockets. Her back is to me while she talks through the intercom. "You can go in for a minute," she says without turning to face me.

A young nurse buzzes me through the door. She and an older nurse are at a command post in the middle of the room with lots of machines. They see each patient through big windows, watch them sleep and breathe. The screens light up, measuring heartbeats and brainwaves.

The young nurse leads me to Eddie's little glass room. He lies in a bed that looks like a crib, with sides that raise and lower. He has tubes in his veins and in his nose. I watch his chest expand and contract with each breath. His dark hair glistens. I lean over his body until my face is in front of his and we breathe the same air. His mouth is relaxed and his eyes are closed.

I place my hand over his eyes. "You don't need to watch me anymore," I whisper in his ear. "I'm okay." My breath shivers. "We were perfect together. I'll always remember." My fingertips are on his eyelids and I feel his eyes moving under my touch. It feels like a baby hummingbird about to break through the shell of its egg. "Get well," I say. "She's waiting for you." I stand there for a while, almost praying.

I walk back out the double doors. The girlfriend stands waiting for me. "He's going to be okay," I tell her.

She lets out a lot of air, and her eyes close for a minute. "I feel it too," she says. She keeps breathing deep. I wait for her to cry. Tears never fall. She opens her eyes and looks at me. She nods her head, rocking back and forth, as if she is carrying a heavy weight around her neck.

....

Later the helmet takes on that nightly glow again. Soft. This time when I look in the face hole, I see his eyes are closed, resting. I fall into a deep sleep and dream of our dancing, our language that no one else speaks.

....

In the morning, I wrap the helmet in my black dress and tie it with gold ribbon, like a present I want to save for later, for some time when I really need it. I lift it way up to the top shelf of my closet. I sigh and feel suddenly alone, released. I take off my robe, then slip a coral-colored dress off a hanger and slide it over my head. I fasten each button with slow, deliberate hands, as if dressing in a new language.

Sandra E. Jones

sue

(excerpt from **The Aunts,** a work in progress)

A year before she died my Aunt Sue rehearsed her death for
her sisters and me. We were at my Aunt Lucy's traditional
New Jersey rancher, relaxing on the patio with lots of leftovers,
iced tea, lemon meringue pie, and the right radio station
playing in the background while we enjoyed a late-August
Sunday afternoon of heavy-duty laughter. A gathering of my
aunts never went longer than ten minutes before it became a
full-fledged theatre and, that Sunday, Sue had star billing.

Sue loved to entertain and to prank people. Her bawdy sense
of comedic delivery matched that of any paid comedian. Aunt
Sue's idea of a good time was to tweak's everyone else's funny
bone while she kept a straight face. Bustling away in her tiny
Philadelphia kitchen, she would tell jokes and stories and
play worn album cuts of routines like "Petey Wheatstraw" and
other highly charged lyrics of standup comedy and blues while
people gorged themselves on her table full of fatty foods.
My aunt's brown eyes could entice you into her huge tales even
before you realized she was spinning one. A master of facial and
physical humor, she knew how to look sad and distraught, how
to stoneface lie, how to bug out those eyes so that it appeared
she had momentarily slipped into madness.

Three of the sisters were in town to attend the funeral of a
classmate. It had been a rather bizarre event. The deceased
was a bit of a clownish figure in life, and in death. Between
outbursts of the man's wives, and his several sets of offspring,
the unflattering toupee and makeup, it had turned out to be
quite the spectacle. Neither the minister nor the choir had
managed to keep a straight face. Sue began by giving us a play
by play of Saturday's service. She ended up giving us a hysterical

rendition of its undertaker and minister. And with those big brown eyes and lopsided wig, she also mastered the deceased.

Inside the cool, dark den Lucy's husband, Carl, sat in his recliner watching sports. We could hear him chuckling along with us. No one was immune to Sue.

Then Sue changed acts. She announced that she would now present her own death scene and funeral. No one seemed bothered by this. She was wearing Carl's barbecue apron. She undid it and went inside. I watched her get another helping of dessert and gather some props on her way to the bathroom.

Aunt Marie, the oldest surviving sister, sat facing outward so she could watch the greenbelt for Mr. Sampson's arrival. Mr. Sampson, a friendly neighbor and Aunt Marie's drinking partner, would probably be strolling along the Willingboro Parkway sidewalk soon with the telltale brown bag.

The two middle sisters, Lucy and Beatrice, sat together in a pale green and white metal glider at one end of the patio opposite the rest of us. They quietly dusted over a few light topics while waiting for Sue to return from her bathroom break.

My mother, ever the industrious and serious one, sat on the patio floor, partly behind Bea and Lucy. This way she could keep a watchful eye on everyone through the latticework of the glider and still carry on her attempts through the screen door to convert Carl.

There is a lapel button often found in card shops that reads: QUICK, LOOK BUSY. JESUS IS COMING. That seemed to be my mother's lifetime motto. She sat multitasking, repotting plants, lining up freshly cleaned garden tools, replenishing lemons and herbal tea. Her board game instructions, her Bible, and an eyeglass repair kit—all next projects in line—leaned against the painted concrete edge.

A stray black and gray dog made his way through the farthest hedges and plopped down in the shade of the shrubbery, ignoring us as though he had ticket reservations. Eventually the dog made eye contact but seemed to want nothing other than our shade and some breeze.

An unusual August wind blew suburban dust-swirls across the concrete and around the buckets of late tomato plants near our waiting audience. I scanned the yard and noticed two magazines opened face down in the grass. About two yards from her battered rubber boots, Mother had prominently displayed copies of *The Watchtower* and *Awake!*, lest we forget "Every opportunity is an opportunity for Jehovah's servant to witness."

One of the pages flipped in the breeze and the dog rose slightly as if beckoned.

Sue danced back outdoors and did a few bits of Richard Pryor and Dolly Parton.

"Ok, let's get to it." Front and center, she froze. She stood there as still as her top-heavy, wheezing smoker's body could be. Then her head began to swivel. She totally got into it. She leaned in to Aunt Marie, way in, their noses almost touching. Quickly passing Lucy and Bea, she whipped around and did the same to me. Just watching her standing there, about to act it all out, was enough. The group of us lost it and Sue hadn't even warmed up. Part mime, part *sotto voce*, she acted out how each one of us would look tiptoeing up on her dead body. She splayed arms in a monstrous pose with clawlike fingers. Her thin, muscled legs bowed above her strappy bronze heels as she concocted gigantic tiptoe steps, holding onto imaginary banisters. Obviously she would die upstairs. A quick jerk of her head in the direction of each one of us indicated who she was going to imitate next. For

nearly an hour she held center stage as she portrayed her death scene and each of our roles in it. She nailed it.

A year later . . .

Bits of the soap from days ago sat alongside her bathtub. Her bathroom smelled of Avon bubble bath, crystals, and oils. Sue had called me over on Friday to help with her bath. Her cough had worsened and her shortened breaths were too precious to waste bathing on her own. The reverb from her gurgling chest was unsettling. Still, she was in her usual good spirits. I scrubbed and swabbed and tried not to think about all the places I had to touch while I tackled the front of her. The room took on the smell of a slightly sweet zoo. After the rinse cycle, Sue startled me by suddenly hoisting a gigantic breast over each shoulder and with her characteristic snaggletoothed grin she said, "You missed a couple of spots. You forgot to towel off the shady side of Titty Town."

The giant mammaries looked like a swollen collar and we made a comedic production of applying talcum powder and then fitting those errant breasts into the new bra prescribed to lessen the pressure on her lungs. Sue did not like the bra.

"I should be wearing my fancy things. This time next year I might not be as sexy. Now honey, do my makeup," she instructed. "And when I die, you make sure I'm looking good for the undertaker. Child, you never know. He might be single!"

That was a longstanding line all my aunts had used. Sue and her sisters often had decreed how they wanted to die, how they wanted to be coiffed and displayed. Each seemed determined to look good and powerful beyond the very end. Sometimes the sisters joked about being buried at some favorite restaurant, or in a car or shocking outfit. Lucy even joked about being buried nude and face down in a glass-topped casket so the world could kiss her posterior goodbye. That always gave these devilishly vain sisters a good laugh.

A few days later, Sue did not answer her phone and I went over to check on her.

At the foot of her silky bed, her death scene was a composition in brown. I found her face down, her coffee bean skin had peeled in a few places and her darkened tongue, swollen and distended, was pressed into the old brown floral carpeting. Her open mouth displayed the missing and yellowed teeth she had worked to disguise in life. The colors in the carpet hinted at the red of her rayon robe and the green of her fluffy mules. The russet shimmer of her hair mirrored the brown in the discolored whites of her eyes. Bronze polish covered similar discolorations in her nails.

It looked like Sue died in a hurry. Without the sponge rollers she wore twenty-four hours a day, Sue was clearly headed somewhere special. Clothes and cosmetics surrounded her. Quilted satin bags with lotions, bath oils, and perfume sets were scattered high and low. I pictured her tabulating and phoning in orders of Avon products. Her corpse seemed caught in sales. At least a dozen fragrances laced together by decay and years of cigarette smoke permeated the room.

I waited until nearly 1:00 AM for the coroner to appear. The older man was polite. His assistant couldn't even spell the word.

"Upstairs or down?" he snapped. I pointed up the stairway and followed them up to her room.

A rapid tug on the zipper and the bag opened. Sticky, then dragging, then flopping sounds followed. A shoe dropped. The thud of Sue's body was followed by the slow closing of the zipper. I stared at the hallway doorjamb. Sue would not have liked these guys, especially the evil-tempered young assistant who was clearly casing the place. My aunt had warned me not to let anyone close her up in some plastic bag. She said she wanted to make sure the neighbors saw her face, since she never hid it while she was alive.

As we headed downstairs, I advised the medical examiner, "Uh, my aunt preferred to have the bag open at the face until inside the wagon." Both men looked at the body bag, then back at me, said nothing, and continued downstairs. Visions of the Atlanta CDC and numerous safety and health protocols and pure logic kept me from repeating the request.

At her funeral, Sue's corpse was impeccable. Things went just as she'd planned. The tributes were all loving and upbeat. The music, the crowd, even the weather would have pleased her. But as we closed the casket, I noticed beneath the cluster of handheld irises that Sue's nails had been painted, not the copper or bronze shades she favored, but a horrible coral. Imagine an Avon lady who hated pink. No, Sue definitely would not have liked this.

Stacy Lawson

putting on the dog

You are not obliged to put on evening clothes to meet God.
—Isaac Bashevis Singer

A Question for the Rebbe

In 2004, I went to Queens, New York, to visit the Lubavitcher Rebbe, Rabbi Menachem Mendel Shneerson. I had come from Seattle with a question for the Rebbe. I wanted to know if we should send Noah, my oldest son, to a secular school or keep him in a Jewish school. If the Rebbe answered a Jewish school, my husband and I wanted to know which one of the three Jewish schools in Seattle. I needed an answer, a sign, a hint, a vision, or a message. We only had two weeks before we had to put down a $2,000 nonrefundable deposit.

I walked into the reception area of a modest brick house on the edge of a cemetery on a steamy spring day. I wore a long, brown skirt, an apple-green long-sleeve top, a pair of bronze boots, and had my hair tucked under a straw hat. Under my arms, were two half-moon sweat stains.

In the reception area men wearing black suits, white shirts, and black hats, and women wearing long skirts, long-sleeve shirts with high necklines, and scarves, hats, or wigs, watched videos of the Rebbe's talks. Some took notes and some wrote letters. Some rocked or swayed as they listened with fierce attention. I sat for a while staring into the Rebbe's clear blue eyes, catching about one out of every four Yiddish words. I took paper and a pen from my small black rubber bag and wrote a note as much to myself as to the Rebbe. It ended with a question. "Should we send Noah to a Jewish school?"

I moved into the next room where there were six long cafeteria tables with people sitting, schmoozing, eating, drinking coffee, sipping tea, and leaning over large volumes of the Talmud rocking and studying in the singsong voice of Torah study. I saw a young couple standing next to each other in a way that implied that they were not brother and sister and, yet, I knew they were not married as the woman's hair was uncovered. I overheard someone say, "They're here for a *bracha* from the Rebbe." I followed them into the back of the room presumably toward the Rebbe where a sign read: PLEASE REMOVE SHOES. I pulled my hot feet out of my boots, lit a candle, and entered the women's side of the *Ohel*, a tent over the Rebbe's gravesite. I recited psalms and quietly read a letter that I had written to the Rebbe. When I finished reading it, I tore it up and let the scraps of paper float down into the plain unadorned concrete square that held other shredded letters above the Rebbe's body. There were bits of notes in Hebrew, Yiddish, Russian, English, French, Farsi, Spanish, and other languages that I didn't recognize. I stayed for at least forty minutes watching people come and go. I watched the young couple, the young woman next to me and the young man across from us on the men's side, praying with fervor, their eyes tightly shut, their lips moving rapidly with an occasional hum escaping. On my way out of the tent, I felt a ping in my left ovary. A sign? Certainly the Rebbe didn't expect me to have another child at forty-three.

I walked out of the house and down a block to where my husband and a friend were waiting for me. In that half a block the human landscape changed from black-hatted Jewish men with their long-sleeved and long-skirted wives to brown, black, tan, and olive-skinned people speaking Spanish. A Hasidic man, with a long black coat, a fur-trimmed hat, and ringlets called *payus* dangling in front of his ears, was behind me speaking rapidly in Yiddish.

"*Bhruklin?* You going to *Bhruklin*?" He asked insistently in English.

Before I realized he was speaking to me, I had pulled off my straw hat and was standing bareheaded scratching my hot scalp. I turned and saw his face fall. It was too late to jam my frizzy-curly hair back under my hat.

"Manhattan," I said. His disgust was palpable.

I climbed into the car carrying the same question that I had when I left Seattle.

Citizen

I wear Citizen jeans and cords—tight, yet, with enough room for my ass and enough fabric to cover my twenty-two-and-a-half-inch thighs. My thighs are larger than my mother's twenty-inch waist was when she married my father in 1950 at the age of twenty.

I'm now forty-eight, five-foot-one-inch, and weigh around 130 pounds. I don't know for sure because we don't own a scale and never have. My husband, for an assortment of reasons, doesn't want a scale, will not discuss weight, or tell me if my ass looks big.

Hence, I've worn the same pants for close to ten years, not just the same size of pants, but literally the same pair of mustard cords and the same pair of black-velvet pants—both by Citizen, bought on the same day in a boutique in Ballard in northwest Seattle. My clothes have always told me what a scale would tell me if I owned one. A month ago, I put my finger through my mustard cords, an inch below the waistband, as I was dragging them over my hips. The other day, I found a hole in the back pocket of my black pants. Now what measure will I use?

Warrior Slays Downward Dog in Lululemon

I started yoga in 1988, before yoga was hip, when only spiritual

seekers, hippies, and the injured were practicing. I started
yoga in a small drafty studio near Green Lake, next to the
Honey Bear Bakery, and close enough to the lake to walk off
my guilt. I started yoga when it was as much about the coffee,
the conversation, and the sour-cream coffeecake as it was about
the postures. I started yoga when a class cost eight dollars, and
there were no such things as yogawear—no yoga pants, no yoga
shirts, no yoga socks, and no yoga skirts. Back then I wore tight
black leggings that made my thighs look like blood sausages
and a baggy T-shirt emblazoned with the logo of some walk,
jog, dance or other-a-*thon*. Now, twenty-three years later,
I shop at Lululemon and pay seventy dollars a pop for a boot-
cut booty-shaping pair of leggings. I wear a black T-shirt on top
of a red, white, brown, navy, or green tank—this ensemble costs
more than one hundred dollars. As far as I can tell it doesn't do
a thing for my poses.

Purim Story No. I
On the Jewish holiday of Purim this year, my husband and I
celebrated our 22nd wedding anniversary. Purim is a story
of good over evil set in ancient Persia with a villain named
Haman, a minister to the king, who is out to annihilate the
Jews. There's King Achashverosh whose wife, Queen Vashti,
has refused to parade naked through the king's grand banquet
and is killed. There's Esther, a closeted Jew, whom the king
chooses to replace Queen Vashti. There's Esther's Uncle
Mordechai, who poses as Esther's father. The story heats up
when Mordechai refuses to bow down to Haman (on account of
an idol hanging from Haman's neck). In the end, Esther, with
coaching from Mordechai, saves her people, Haman is killed,
Mordechai is honored by the king, and Esther becomes known
as the savior of the Jewish people. The holiday is celebrated
with community revelry, a recitation of the story, a donning
of costumes, fasting, eating, pranking, playing tricks, and
for some, drinking until one is unable to tell the difference
between blessed Mordechai and cursed Haman.

This year, I decided to surprise my husband and dress as Queen Vashti. I took my calf-length ivory-lace wedding dress out of the closet, dropped my leggings, pulled off my T-shirt, bunched the dress up and put it over my head. I slid it down over one shoulder than the other. I wriggled my arms into the sleeves and began inching the three-layer dress over my boobs, a single layer at a time. I sucked in my gut and willed my hips to narrow. I eased the fabric with my fingertips over my curves, contours, bulges, and dips. I sucked in a final time, knit my ribs together, and struggled with the zipper. I got it halfway up when it occurred to me that the dress might fit better with the proper undergarments. I unzipped, grabbed the bottom of the dress—rolled it back over my belly, hips, thighs, boobs, and up to my shoulders when it got stuck. "Steve! Steve!" I called. No response. I walked downstairs in my black underwear and black socks, holding onto the oak banister, with the dress over my head.

"I need help," I yelled this time.

"I'll say you do. Boys should we leave your mother this way?"

"Sure," Noah giggled.

"No. That's not nice," my youngest son Shiah said.

"How the heck did you do this?" Steve asked as he tried to free me.

Careful," I said through the ivory-lace layers wrapped around my head.

Steve inched the fabric up and off of me while suggesting that the dress must have shrunk in the closet. I sulked back upstairs in my black socks and underwear with my dress over my shoulder. I examined the dress in the bathroom. The shoulders had ridiculously thick shoulder pads. Without them, I decided I'd have more room for my arms. I took out fingernail scissors and began cutting the satin on the inside of the dress until I had a hole large enough to excise the wad of cotton batting. I put on a pair of tight black bike shorts to hold in my midsection and took off my bra and let my boobs down.

Again, I dropped the dress over my head, gathered the fabric in my hands and lowered it over my shoulders and on down until I was in and zipped. One look in the mirror told me to get out quickly.

Seminary

In 1979, I left Seattle for *Neveh Yerushaliem,* a women's seminary in Israel with my best friend Patti Calderon *zikhronha l'vrakha* of blessed memory. I was seventeen and had just graduated from high school. Patti was a year older and had been in New York for a year at Stern College. We left for the airport directly from our friend Ann's wedding. Ann, also of blessed memory, had begged us to dance at her wedding before we left.

Patti and I arrived in Jerusalem on a suffocating August day. We were in the land of the holy, in a religious girls' school, and we were required to dress modestly at all times. Patti had a large lovely chest and no matter what she wore, she drew attention. I on the other hand had no such issues. I filled a 32A cup if I leaned forward and squeezed my upper arms into the sides of my chest.

One day as I was leaving *Pirkei Avot,* Ethics of Our Fathers class, the teacher (whose name I have long forgotten) asked to speak to me. She was a beautiful, tall, reedy woman wearing a long-tailored dress that looked like it came from a Talbot's catalog.

"Yocheved, may I speak to you for a moment?"

"Sure," I answered a bit surprised.

"I know that you are a religious girl," she began, "so I want to tell you that your shirt is too tight and is immodest."

I was wearing an off-white knit turtleneck with a white bra underneath. The sleeves went to my wrists and the collar to my chin. Never had I thought about anything being too tight on me.

I have no idea what I said, but I rushed back to tell the girls at the dorm about my scolding. For months, I had been perfecting my imitation of this teacher and, now, I had new material to work. Back in my room, I stared at the mirror, squinted, turned to the side. I saw nothing—not the faintest outline of a nipple, not a wrinkle, and barely a wave in the fabric as it curved around my breasts.

Purim Story No. 2
This past Purim—the same Purim that found me attempting to slip into my ivory-lace wedding dress as the reincarnated, lovely, and liberated Queen Vashti—I arrived at a Belltown condo for a *Megillah* reading and Purim cocktail party wearing my black cords (now with holes in both back pockets), a white long-sleeve T-shirt (because I don't own a white blouse), a grey tie, a black jacket, and a black Fedora.

I had pulled out a bit of hair from behind each ear, wetted the clumps and twisted them around my index fingers. I pinned both sections above my ears to dry. When I removed the bobby pins, I had two perfect *payus* that fell down the sides of my face. I put on a black Fedora that I bought from a thrift store and a touch of black honey lip gloss and left the house looking like a prepubescent boy from Brooklyn.

Baby & Co.

Baby Burstyn was my first and only fashion idol. I first set eyes
on her at synagogue in the early seventies when I was around
fourteen, and she was probably in her late twenties. She wore
black fishnet hose, tight short black dresses in sheer fabrics,
plunging necklines, asymmetrical hemlines, black platform
shoes, and black suede boots. She let her long, black curly hair
swing freely while most of the married women wore hats, wigs,
lace mantillas, and scarves to cover their hair as was the custom
of the congregation. Baby was a walking affront to the row of
wealthy handsome women in veiled hats wearing charcoal,
black, and navy blue suits.

Baby was sexy and wild and round and unpredictable and
unpretentious and unafraid to wear whatever she wanted. She
wore skirts with leggings before anyone knew what leggings
were. Her style was French and witty and beautiful and ironic
and artistic and original. When she and her husband Uri
opened Baby & Co. in 1976, a high-end boutique at the corner
of First and Virginia, I was in high school. I counted the years
until I had enough money to make my first purchase, a long
printed batik Vivienne Tam skirt—inky-blue and off-white with
a black layer of the same crepe material underneath. I've worn
it through two pregnancies, one bris, countless parties, and
twenty years later, I'm still wearing it.

Purim Story No. 3

At the Belltown Purim party, I watched a tall lithe woman in
a body-skimming frosted blue dress, black fishnet hose, and
a pair of black pumps with a considerable heel. She had short
platinum blonde hair worn in a flip. When she turned around,
I saw she was a he.

Across the room was a tall big-boned brunette woman who was
leaning against a wall with her partner. Her face was long, her

nose sharp, her hands large, her voice low, and her skin a bit rough. She was dressed in a skirt, blouse, and sweater vest. She had once been Mark and now she was Miriam. A beautiful statement of change—refreshingly normal and open about what she had been through to become a woman.

When I told my friend Roz about the costumes and alterations, she said, "Strict gender identity is giving way. Younger people are more flexible."

Thread Count

When I was young my mother worked for my father's family business, Lawson Manufacturing, a coat company headquartered on Bellevue Avenue on Capitol Hill. The coats they made were wool, cashmere, and camel hair. They were sold at Nordstrom, Frederick & Nelson, and I. Magnin. When I was a kid, before the start of every school year, I would go to the factory, and my Uncle Harry would lift me onto the cutting table and size me for a new coat. I'd go on my way with a new navy peacoat or a camel-hair coat.

Somewhere I learned to rub material between my thumb and forefinger to detect synthetic blends. In Israel in the Jerusalem Arab Market I learned to light a match to a corner of fabric. If it went up in flames it was not a natural fabric. I look at buttons, buttonholes, and zippers with the careful eye of a jeweler before I buy anything. My mother's mother was also the daughter of a tailor. She would inspect seams and shake her head if there was a single loose thread or a sloppy line.

Torah Dressing

I bought a Torah on Ebay for $6,500 for a new Jewish community that I helped to create. The Torah was written in Poland before the Second World War, made its way to Ramat Gan in Israel after the war, and on a Saturday morning in February 2007 arrived on my front porch in a box that was torn and dented. Noah and I ran down to the rabbi's house with a question. What does one do with a Torah that arrives on Shabbas in a busted-up box?

The Torah's red velvet mantle was frayed, the wooden rollers were broken, the parchment worn in areas, and letters had rubbed off from use. We hired a *sofer,* a scribe and Torah repair-person from Israel, to come to Seattle to perform the repairs. She arrived with a quill, ink, and *gid*, kosher sinew, required to sew the parchment.

This year we're working with an artist in Chicago to create a new mantle. We're measuring, sizing, sketching, designing, and selecting fabric, trim, and thread. The process is as involved, exacting, and as expensive as having a dress made to order.

Sandra E. Jones

you have cancer

It was okay,

Hearing it with an audience,

Receiving it

Cold and methodically. Immediately

Enraged at its sneaky intrusion,

I sensed that I could beat it.

Having him tell me that way

Called out

My interior warrior performer,

Making it real. A viable enemy yes,

But not the total threat

Had this news arrived by letter,

Inside some deceptively bland,

White envelope

With a clear window

To the end of one's life.

Janet Yoder

healing heart symphony

Seattle. Saturday afternoon, May 20, 2006. The people are going there. To Benaroya Hall. They are going there to hear the Healing Heart Symphony.

We gather in the outer hall, under the Chihuly glass chandelier, an opulent knot of pearlescent tentacles. Smell of Starbucks. Our breath comes fast, as if we had been chasing this day for a year, or longer. People wear their finery: suits, flowing dresses, necklaces of amber and dentalium, Pendleton wool vests and jackets, best flannel shirts, a boutonniere and a rain hat—both woven of cedar bark. We see people we know and love and too seldom see. Squeal of a beloved name. Hug. Kiss. Camera click.

Is Vi here? We strain to see who gets off the elevators from the parking garage. Finally, it is Vi. Her vision is mostly gone; she holds niece Carmen's arm lightly, as if held aloft purely by anticipation. Vi, at 88, has become tiny. Her hair is short and still mostly dark. Her face is small behind her eyeglasses, giving her the look of a wise child. Her voice is like a sprinkle of rain, the kind of voice that makes you want to listen. Now, her long-awaited day has arrived, the end of a sweet journey of expectation. Vi embraces one person after another, enfolding each of us in the drape of her soft red shawl.

"Aren't we lucky?" Vi beams. "We get to hear *our* symphony today." She doesn't say it is her symphony, though she commissioned it; nor does she say it is Bruce Ruddell's, though he composed it. It is ours. And the world's.

◆ ◆

First Movement: Prepare

Small shakers begin a heartbeat. Alone. Then violins join, ocean harp, and temple gong: sustain, diminuendo. Soprano sax sings the melody, plaintive like an Indian Shaker Church song. The vocalist enters in unison. No words. Violins rise and call like a voice. Breathy flute, like water caught in an eddy. Crescendo. Fortissimo. Then release, until only the bass and piano remain. Strike. Hold. Fade.

Vi Hilbert is an Upper Skagit tribal elder. Her parents spoke Lushootseed, the language Chief Seattle spoke, the language that describes the world of Puget Sound from the Skagit River down to Squaxin Island, the language that names Elk, Beaver, Deer, Eagle, Mink, Bear, and tells of their deeds, good and bad. As a child, Vi took in this world: stories, Longhouse speeches, Indian Shaker Church songs, secret talk between her folks, even gossip—all in Lushootseed. As an adult, she learned that her childhood language was dying; she made it her life work to keep it alive.

Vi could have gone down the path of traditional healers. She could have become an Indian Doctor, like her most revered relatives. She could have entered Longhouse life, received her song, and danced her spirit dance. She could have gone into the Indian Shaker Church to become a spiritual leader. But Vi's father told her she was not to do any of that: "You have work that you will do, Daughter." So, she resisted the callings, resisted the spirit songs that came to her, resisted the dreams that pulled her toward that world. Instead, she worked on her language, stories, oral histories, and cultural teachings. Instead, she taught hundreds and spoke to thousands. She shared what she knew. This work was placed on her in a sacred way. A gift.

❖ ❖

Some gathering here have been Vi's students. Some are tribal people. Some were skeptical this symphony would come to pass. Some have been in her world a long time and know that when Vi wants something done, it gets done.

"I want to commission a symphony, Bruce, but I have no money," Vi told composer Bruce Ruddell in 2002. Word had gone out that Vi was looking for a composer. Ellen Mae, one of Vi's volunteers, told her husband, Larry Blain. Larry played viola with the Bremerton Symphony. That orchestra commissioned and performed a piece by Bruce Ruddell in 2001 called *13 Soundbytes for Spring*. Larry and Ellen went to visit Bruce in Canada, learned that Bruce had collaborated with the esteemed Haida artist, Bill Reid, to create an oratorio to tell the story of Mr. Reid's sculptural masterpiece, *The Spirit of Haida Gwaii*. Bruce Ruddell was a composer who had already journeyed in Indian Country.

"There's somebody I'd like you to meet down here," Larry told Bruce over the phone a couple of weeks after their visit in Canada. That was all Bruce knew when Larry and Ellen brought him and his family to Vi Hilbert's home.

"They introduced us to Vi and left!" Bruce said. "So we sat around Vi's table for seven hours, without a break. She had us in tears, and entertained. At the end of those seven hours, she said that she had a dream, a vision, in which two sacred songs needed to inspire a symphonic work so that the power of those songs could start working again. She said, 'I want you to do this.' So that is how it happened."

"I have no money," Vi told Bruce. Instead, she offered spirit songs: a Thunder Power song from Chief Seattle, entrusted to Vi by his descendants; and a Healing Song, bestowed upon her by her beloved cousin, Isadore Tom (Indian name: pətius), at the end of his life. "Use it when you need it, cousin," pətius told her.

❖ ❖

The events of September 11 made Vi sick at heart, and she knew the time had come. Vi placed these songs in the heart of the Healing Heart Symphony. She tendered them to Bruce Ruddell on cassette tapes. "They sat on my desk for some time while I tried to figure out how I would actually approach something like this," Bruce said of the tapes. "So then one day, I took them in my backpack, along with a portable cassette machine. I went for a climb up Mt. Erskine on Salt Spring Island. It's a beautiful climb up to the top, a great place to think or to just be. I listened to them there at the top of this mountain. It was a beautiful day. I listened to them twice each, no more than that. Then I put them aside, and I didn't listen to them again. At that time, the form of the piece came pretty quickly."

The songs cannot be quoted in the music. "Or," as Vi says, "the shit would hit the fan." A song is owned by a family. Others can hear the song, sing it, even be healed by the song. But the song belongs to the family. So, Vi asked Bruce to compose a symphony inspired by these spirit songs, sacred songs, songs of the healing heart. "The Seattle Symphony is going to play it," Vi told Bruce, "and you will be paid properly." At the time, she had no agreement from the Seattle Symphony; and, as she oft repeated, "I have no money."

So, other people worried about the money for Vi's symphony. Larry and Ellen drummed up money, some from their own pockets. My husband, Robby, and I gave a little money. Friends of Vi's tucked money into her Pendleton wool handbag or slid money inside letters. Money came from the Seattle Foundation. Money came from the Tulalip Tribe because their casino success allows them to support the culture. Money travels in Indian Country. People shake hands with money and leave cash in someone's palm, or slip folded bills into the breast pocket of a flannel shirt.

❖ ❖

With this money, two movements of the symphony were
composed; then the money ran out. Vi refused to worry about
the money. She remembers, as a girl, selling fish at the kitchen
doors of white ladies' houses. "You want to buy a fish?" She
felt like she was begging. Vi won't beg for money. She believes
money will come. "Lushootseed takes care of itself," she says.
The Lushootseed monetary mantra repeats like a line of music,
like the symphony itself.

In summer 2002, we came to Vi's house in Seattle to hear those
first two movements. We sat on sofas, armchairs, and dining
chairs lined up in her living room, as if it were a small concert
hall. Patricia Kim came as envoy of the Seattle Symphony.
Bruce Ruddell stood in front of us. In a soft voice, he explained
that the sounds we would hear were computer-generated and
not as rich or distinct as an orchestra. His face flushed, as if he
fought an urge to say more. He pushed the play button on Vi's
boom box and sat down.

We listened. At times, the music rose to a continuous sound
that I imagined would require much of the wind players.
The score directs them to "stagger breathing." Maybe money
is like the air that blows from the musician's mouth into the
mouthpiece and on down the grenadilla wood of the clarinet
and oboe, or the silver metal of flute, or through the rosy brass
of trumpet, trombone, French horn. Shared, there is enough
air, enough to keep the sound coming. And the strings bow
steadily, changing direction with no break in sound. And it all
keeps coming, as much as is needed, for as long as it is needed.

Word travels that money is short. People know people who
might give money: the Tudor Foundation. They do give money.
In April 2003, the symphony is written. In May 2005, Maestro
Gerard Schwarz decides the Seattle Symphony Orchestra will
perform it. Now, May 20, 2006, we gather for the premiere of
the Healing Heart Symphony.

❖ ❖

Second Movement: Thunder Spirit Power Song

*The percussionist lifts Vi's father's drum into the air. The drum is named
Captain and bears a soaring eagle. The drummer beats a slow, steady pulse
that gathers the musicians one by one. When all are present, the music rises to
voluminous sound, then calms, then builds again. Wind arpeggios fly. Full
orchestra plays full chords. Building to thick thunder, to rolling, roiling, rising
sound. Drop. Then rise again, to the last three chords.*

We enter the inner lobby and look out the wall of windows at
our glistening city: glass, steel, stone, saltwater. We gather in
small groups that shift, then shift again, like slivers of colored
glass in a kaleidoscope.

Johnny Moses steps to the center of the lobby. Nearing
40, Johnny is a small man with a huge voice. Johnny is Vi's
nephew, a brilliant storyteller, and an Indian Doctor who
carries the name Walking Medicine Robe. He sometimes has
his troubles: a couple of his front teeth are now broken, and
his face shows faded bruises of a recent beating that he says
happened one night right here, in front of Benaroya Hall.
By asking him to address the crowd, "to lay the carpet of
spiritual understanding," Vi calls up the sublime best of
Johnny. He speaks of his Auntie, of the symphony, of the place
where we are standing. "This land we are on is sacred. This
was a burial ground here." He points down through the floor.
"There's work that needs to be done." He sings Indian Shaker
Church songs, whose melodies rise like the most familiar
Sunday hymns. We all join voice.

Vi gives assignments. Some are general: She exhorts her audi-
ences to listen to the story of Lady Louse and, in response, to
create their own stories of how this petite insect person got

◈ ◈

lost. For her 75th birthday at the Upper Skagit Reservation, Vi asked each guest to adopt a traditional story, memorize it (if possible in Lushootseed), stand and tell the story at her party, then become the story's guardian. Now, she asks her circle of people to write how *The Earth Is Our First Teacher;* collected, these will become a book. Other assignments are for specific people: create a Lushootseed textbook, a dictionary, or a book of the stories from when animals were people, or of Lushootseed place names throughout Puget Sound. Or produce a documentary film. Curate a show of cedar bark baskets. Even compose a symphony.

In Indian Country, Vi is known for commissioning work. She had Alice Williams of Upper Skagit make her a cedar bark dress, now on display at the Seattle Art Museum. She asked Ora Parent of Makah to string "Happy Bead" necklaces, named for the clicking of beads against olivella shells when the wearer moves. Vi commissioned Fran and Bill James of Lummi to weave her a thick wool blanket in traditional design. Vi commissions work to support the artists monetarily, to give recognition and praise; and she commissions work to have the pleasure of giving these treasures to people she loves.

Vi arranges for a tribal fisherman to catch salmon for her birthday party. She supports his fishing business, and then offers the salmon, roasted on sticks staked in front of an open fire, to all of her friends and family. This commission is given for dinner, along with Skagit corn on the cob, sliced tomatoes that her husband grew, and mountain blackberry cobbler.

All sorts of things move around Indian Country: baskets, blankets, shawls, jewelry, carved cedar. Vi might receive a blanket as a gift and pass it on to its new owner within the month. Given, and given again, these objects gain value and accrete meaning.

❖ ❖

A commission is a gift. So are assignments. Once, I edited
a book for Vi, a collection of Lady Louse stories that Vi had
assigned everyone to write. In the original story, Lady Louse
got lost cleaning her house where she lived all alone. Our
27-year-old illustrator received a diagnosis of a serious cancer.
The illness set him adrift, and I wondered if we should release
him from the assignment of illustrating. Vi spotted the young
man when she was speaking to a crowd at Seattle Bookfest. She
had him stand, and she introduced him as "my illustrator."
She announced the book would be out in December and asked
him if he would have the drawings of Lady Louse ready. "Yes,"
he answered. I don't know what it required of him, but he got
them in as promised: subtle, laconic drawings in which Lady
Louse gets so lost that we see only what she has left behind.
We celebrated the book's release with dinner at a Belltown café.
Vi spoke words of intimate gratitude to the young man; the
splendor of his smile told me that she had known exactly what
she was doing.

Vi receives her own assignments from her ancestors. "My folks
speak to me here." She points at the white wooden altar with
its white cross in front of her living room window. "They tell
me what I need to do." I look at Vi's altar and I wonder what it
means to get assignments from the Other Side, from the
Spirit World.

Vi's ancestors told her to heal through music. Music has a wider
reach than words, especially words only spoken in Western
Washington's Puget Sound, and not even all of that. Bruce
Ruddell stepped up to receive this assignment. When asked why
she commissioned a symphony, Vi joked, "Because I'm a bossy
old Indian." In fact, she was doing the work given to her, and
the work was healing her.

Third Movement: Healing Song
The Longhouse drum rolls as if to accompany a dancer's cry as his song comes on him. Soprano sax enters with the song, passes it on to others, then receives it again. The Longhouse drum begins a steady beat, like an Indian Doctoring song. Gentle power. Sustain. Phrases step down to close, bless, and heal.

We enter the concert hall as if it is hallowed: a Cathedral or a Longhouse. Vi sits up front to listen to her spirit songs travel in a new canoe, deep inside a new work. The songs are now carried in the heart of the symphony. Or perhaps the songs carry the symphony. Vi's gift makes it possible. Why do some people give away what they value most, while others hoard it?

I remember Vi telling the story of Swallow, which comes from Tulalip Elder Hariette Shelton Dover. Vi gave the story her own twist: Swallow was living there with all the other birds. The Changer came and saw that the birds had no homes. So, he told them to build their homes. He showed them how to do it, how to make their nests. All did as directed, except for Swallow, who swished about, dressed up in her feather headband and bright beads, showing off her treasures. Then it was time for the Changer to come back and see all the birds' new homes. But Swallow didn't have a home; she didn't even know how to build one. So, she took some mud and quickly made a house out of that mud. She built it big enough to hold all her treasures. She pulled her beads, jewels, and shiny bits inside her house. Then she mudded up the opening to protect her prizes. The next morning, the mud had hardened and Swallow couldn't get out. Poor Mud Swallow—stuck inside there with all her treasures.

❖ ❖

Every time I visit Vi now at her apartment in La Conner, Washington, she gives me something. As I prepare to leave, she reaches for a paper she helped write for a museum catalog, or she goes to her curio cabinet to find a small basket, or to her entry closet to pull out a shawl. The second time she offers me a shawl, I resist. I take her hand and remind her she has already given me one, that I am honored to wear this beautiful reminder of her. She goes to the closet anyway. "Your mother might need this." She places the soft alpaca wool in my hands. So I accept; now my mother wears this shawl. Last time I visited Vi, we talked about the symphony, and then, as I gathered my tape recorder, she insisted on loaning me the music score.

You would think Vi's little apartment would be empty by now, with all the treasures Vi places in the hands of her visitors. But somehow treasures replenish. Visitors bring her gifts: pints of fresh strawberries, a triple bouquet of daffodils, a CD of Elvis tunes. At gatherings throughout Indian Country, Vi routinely receives a blanket or even a nobility robe of mountain goat wool, to thank her for speaking, or just for being there. Plus, Vi loves to buy things from Indian basket weavers, from her daughter's alpaca ranch boutique, or from quilters who are her neighbors at the La Conner Retirement Inn.

Fourth Movement: The Journey Forward

Slow Longhouse drumbeat. Vocalist speaks the text in Lushootseed, sounds stretching out, a recitation of credo. Falling lines in flute and strings against rising lines in the piano. Wind triplets. Soprano sax melody. Then faster, with a gathering strength. Arpeggios build to thunder power. Then a key change. Shift to healing. Lush horns. Glockenspiel rings like Indian Shaker altar bells. Continuous sound of prayer. Stagger breathing. Share air. Share sound. Lushootseed blessing: ʔi yabid tiʔəʔ səliʔ. haydxʷ kʷi xaʔx̌aʔ. gʷəkʷaxʷacid. Honor the spirit. Know the sacred. It will help you!

◈ ◈

We sit in Benaroya Hall and let the music work on us. The four
movements make their journey around the four directions and
around the seasons; four is the sacred number in Lushootseed.
For a year, we have carried this date, the anticipation of this
music, and Vi's intentions. We have carried them close to us.
For a year, we have borne the fragility of our elders; we have
lost Vi's husband and then her son. For a year, our gatherings
have been in grief. For a year, we have waited. Now, the Healing
Heart pierces my heart. I am grateful to be here, grateful Vi is
still with us, grateful to receive this music, this gift.

I consider gifts: Chief Seattle's gift of welcome to the arriving
pioneers; and the gift of Vi's cousin pətius, a renowned Indian
Doctor, who got up from his own hospital bed because he was
called to go do a healing on someone. I think about Vi's gift of
this symphony. I think about giving, even when it seems little or
nothing comes back. Or does it all come back?

"People that have passed on into other worlds are there to
honor the gift," Vi says. "This symphony includes them, even
though they are on the Other Side. I think this is the unspoken
gift, that people on the Other Side are always with us to support
the work."

The last sound releases into air. The Healing Heart Symphony
settles over us. I will its message into memory, direct it deep
into my marrow to regenerate and enrich my blood for the
years to come, for the years when, if I am so lucky, I will receive
assignments from the Other Side.

THE END

notes about the writers

Carol Bolt

Carol is a visual artist, writer, and chef. She mostly hangs her hat in the Pacific Northwest but loves an adventure in her camper van: Big Blue. She is best known in the visual arts community for teaming up with fellow artists to start two Seattle galleries: SOIL Artists' Cooperative and Platform Gallery. As a writer she is best known for her series "*The Book of Answers*" published by Hyperion and Stewart, Tabori & Chang. As a chef, it's her kick-ass cookies. Please find more information at www.thebookofanswers.com and www.Carolbolt.com.

Pamela Hobart Carter

Growing up American in Montreal gave Pam a great French accent and an outsider's take. For more than twenty-five years she has been teaching everything from preschool to science pedagogy, mostly in Seattle. She lives with her husband and two teenagers. Live Girls! selected her first full-length script, *Rondo*, to read in their new works festival in 2008. In 2009, North Seattle Community College produced *It's Not in the P-I*, a play Pam co-wrote with five other locals. She also writes poems (one in *Barrow Street*) and short shorts (one in *Quick Fiction*) and climbs plastic.

Geri Gale

Geri Gale lives in Seattle. Her poetry and prose have appeared in *Bayou Magazine, Raven Chronicles, Otoliths, Canadian Jewish Outlook*, and *Under the Sun* (forthcoming). Her major works include: *Patrice: A Poemella*; a collection of prosepoems, *She*; and a coming-of-age screenplay, *Swayed*.

Sandra E. Jones

A member of Seattle's Teahouse Kuan Yin Writers since 1992, which grew into the current Uptown Writers group, Sandra's work has been noted in local spoken-word appearances at Seattle's Hugo House, OK Hotel Poetry Slams, and at Red Sky productions. Author Terri Casey featured Sandra's poem "Ladybug" in her book *Pride and Joy: The Lives and Passions of Women Without Children* (2001). In 1997, Sandra's stories and poetry were also featured by the Seattle arts organization SOIL and the Los Angeles POST Theatre. Jones has volunteered as a teacher in the Seattle School District's Powerful Writers literacy program. She takes great delight in humor, witty exchanges, and in having the smartest friends in the universe.

Susan Knox

Susan Knox lives in a downtown Seattle condominium overlooking Elliott Bay, just north of the Pike Place Market where she shops most days for fish and vegetables, wine, and cheese. Her book *Financial Basics: A Money Management Guide for Students* was published by the Ohio State University Press and her essay, *"Remember Me,"* appeared in the Winter 2009 issue of the *Pisgah Review* and *CALYX* (forthcoming).

Stacy Lawson

Stacy Lawson is a yoga instructor and writer living in Seattle with her husband and two young sons. She is the founder of Red Square Yoga, a collaborative yoga studio. She is a dedicated writing student of Priscilla Long whose generosity of time, spirit, and inspiration is overwhelming. Stacy's work has appeared in *Under the Sun* and *Drash: Northwest Mosaic*.

Arleen Williams

Arleen has recorded her life in journals since she left home and began her wanderings in her late teens. Decades later those journals filled the gaps where memory alone failed, making possible Arleen's first book, *The Thirty-Ninth Victim* (Blue Feather Books, LTD., 2008), a memoir that tells the story of her family's journey before and after her sister was murdered by the worst serial killer in American history. Arleen's short memoir pieces appeared in *Crosscurrents* (WCCHA, 2009), *In Our Prime* (2010), and, on occasion, at www.arleenwilliams.com. Arleen lives and writes, walks and teaches in West Seattle.

Janet Yoder

Janet Yoder lives with her husband Robby Rudine on their Seattle houseboat. She is a member of the musical group, Batucada, which plays traditional Brazilian and Caribbean music. Her writing has appeared in *Raven Chronicles, Bayou, Porcupine, Passager, The MacGuffin, North Dakota Quarterly, The Evansville Review, The Massachusetts Review, Pilgrimage, River Teeth, Chautauqua,* and *Signs of Life*. She is currently at work on a collection of personal essays about Skagit tribal elder, Vi Hilbert. She has been writing with the Uptown Writers for eighteen years.

acknowledgments

Writing a book is full of mystery. Many parts make the whole. We come to the Uptown Espresso table with pen and paper and coffee and imagination; still, without the help and support of others we might not have made our Sunday morning treks to writing practice. We would like to thank our community of supporters who nourished the making of our art—our family, our friends, and our writing associates, teachers, mentors, and other inspiring artists.

We want to thank the terrific baristas at the Uptown Espresso, as well as Dow Lucurell, president. We appreciate your delicious coffee, great service, and the generosity of allowing us to write every Sunday morning at your Seattle locations at 2504 Fourth Avenue and 500 Westlake Avenue North.

Distinguished writers and brilliant teachers, Robert J. Ray and Jack Remick, have taught many of us the spirit of Natalie Goldberg's timed-writing practice. Through the years Robert and Jack have generously taught us the power of writing to the thirty-one-minute clock at Louisa's Café & Bakery at 2379 Eastlake Avenue East, Seattle. Some of us study with the superb writer and extraordinary teacher Priscilla Long.

We offer our gracious thanks to our family, loved ones, and friends: Bob and Doris Bolt, Carol Bolt, Jocelyn Bridges, Christie Brown, Muriel Curtis, Gabriel Dehlendorf, Roth Dehlendorf, Leah Elgin, Elsie Yoder Forest, Alex Gale, Patricia E. Gale, Jaclynn Hiranaka, Dylan Hirshkowitz, Malya Hirshkowitz, Roy Hirshkowitz, Kim Howard, Jane Ihrig, Madison Ihrig, Todd Ihrig, Weldon Ihrig, the Jones family, Sandra Everlasting Jones, David Karachuk, Kyle Karachuk, Alan Knox, Deborah Knox, Drake Knox, James Knox, Sloane Knox, Patty Kunitsugu, Luisa Motten, Scott Parducci, Jodi Pilatowski, Ron Pilatowski, Robby Rudine, Noah Sarkowsky, Shiah Sarkowsky, Steve Sarkowsky, Erin Williams, Lucy Williams, Tom Williams, Janet Yoder, and Josie Zhuo.

Special recognition to all of our teachers, mentors, other writers, artists: Joel Chafetz, Billie Condon, Lori DeMarre, Irene Drennan, Nikki Giovanni, Natalie Goldberg, Layne Goldsmith, Gay Hadley, Don Harmon, Kate Holcomb, Jim Karnitz, Jean Lenihan, Susan Little, Priscilla Long, Donald McKinlay, Michael Mendonsa, Paul Mullin, Suzanne Murray, Jo Nelson, Annette Niemtzow, Deborah Pursifull, Judith van Praag, Robert J. Ray, Francia Recalde, Jack Remick, Laurel Richardson, Portia Hamilton Sperr, Stewart Stern, Anne Sweet, Pat Takayama, Diana Taylor, Jane Vollbrecht, Gordon Wood, and all the writers who meet at Louisa's Café & Bakery every Tuesday and Friday afternoon to put pen to paper and read around the tables. Carol Bolt says: "Thank you to all my Uptown writing comrades. You are a great source of Inspiration and Spirit. I am grateful for the Sunday morning seat that you save for me and that it's okay if I show up in jeans and a T-shirt and not the scratchy dress."

We also want to express our gratitude to our editor, Waverly Fitzgerald, and our designer, Pamela Farrington, for enhancing our words and taking our collaborative effort to the next level of artistry.

6242720R0

Made in the USA
Charleston, SC
01 October 2010